The Flavors of

BON APPÉTIT

2006

Lemon Chiffon Layer Cake with Candied Rose Petals
(page 206)

The Flavors of
BON APPÉTIT
2006

from the Editors of Bon Appétit

Condé Nast Books

New York

For *Bon Appétit* Magazine

Barbara Fairchild, *Editor-in-Chief*
Tricia Callas O'Donnell, *Contributing Editor, Books*
Marcy MacDonald, *Editorial Operations Director*
Carri Marks Oosterbaan, *Editorial Production Director*
Michelle Alderson, *Editorial Production Manager*
Sybil Shimazu Neubauer, *Editorial Administrator*
Marcia Hartmann Lewis, *Editorial Support*
Susan Champlin, *Text*
Shayna Sobol, *Copy Editor*
Karen Hallal, *Research*
Elizabeth A. Matlin, *Index*

For Condé Nast Books

Lisa Faith Phillips, *Vice President and General Manager*
Tom Downing, *Direct Marketing Director*
Deborah Williams, *Operations Director*
Lyn Barris Hastings, *Associate Marketing Director*
Eric Killer, *Assistant Marketing Manager*
Angela Donadic, *Marketing Assistant*

Design: Monica Elias and Ph.D

Front Jacket: Chili-Garlic Shrimp with Mixed Greens, Avocado, and Corn (page 99)
Facing Page: Top: Seared Sea Scallops with Banyuls Vinegar and Chicory Slaw (page 12)
         Middle: Herb-Brined Pork Loin Rib Roast (page 62)
         Bottom: Lemon Meringue Blueberry Pie (page 180)

Published by Condé Nast Books, Random House Direct, Inc., New York, New York.
A wholly owned subsidiary of Random House, Inc.

Printed in the United States of America

Library of Congress Cataloging-in-Publication Data is available upon request.

10 9 8 7 6 5 4 3 2 1

FIRST EDITION

Condé Nast Web Address: bonappetit.com
Bon Appétit Books Web Address: bonappetitbooks.com

Contents

Introduction

What is it you want most as you approach a brand-new cookbook? You probably want to know that the recipes are creative, delicious, doable, foolproof, and that they'll wow all of your friends.

So let's cut to the chase: The recipes in *The Flavors of Bon Appétit 2006* are creative, delicious, doable, foolproof—and all of them will definitely wow all of your friends. In other words, these recipes are pure *Bon Appétit*.

From Roasted Red Pepper and Feta Dip (page 20) to Chocolate-Orange Pots de Crème with Candied Orange Peel (page 214), these recipes represent the very best of *Bon Appétit*'s signature style. They are sophisticated, fresh, and fun, combining your favorite flavors with exciting new ingredients and techniques that bring the whole world into your kitchen.

You'll find all the foods you love to cook with, shown off in inspiring new presentations. Here is that versatile wild salmon fillet, now served with a fantastic accompaniment of peas and pea tendrils tossed in a lemon dressing (page 90). Then there's everyone's weeknight staple, the simple chicken breast, transformed with a kicky pistachio-cilantro pesto (page 75). And isn't that the classic potato salad dressed up with prosciutto and truffle oil (page 158)? Pure *Bon Appétit*.

Every issue of the magazine offers an array of the great flavors of the world, adapted in ingenious ways for the home cook. Our editors, writers, recipe developers, testers, and tasters

Salmon with Peas, Pea Tendrils, and Dill-Cucumber Sauce (page 90)

find inspiration everywhere: in the seasonal fruits and vegetables available at farmers' markets across the country; in the innovative repertoires of standout young chefs; in the culinary traditions of the many countries to which we travel.

Inspiration comes from another source, too: *Bon Appétit* readers. You are as passionate and opinionated as we are—and, let us say, you're not shy about sharing. You tell us all about the foods you love, the ways you entertain, the restaurants that have inspired you, the dishes you're eager to try.

So when it comes time to gather the best recipes of the year, we look for the ones that represent everything the magazine is about: classic style, contemporary approach, extraordinary results. This encompasses everything from quick-and-clever dishes you can whip up on a

Chocolate-Orange Pots de Crème with Candied Orange Peel (page 214)

weeknight or on a whim—think Mustard-Seed-Crusted Burgers with Horseradish Slaw (page 45)—to more complex combinations of ingredients, like Shrimp Curry with Yu Choy and Kabocha Squash (page 101), in which the beautiful, mildly bitter Asian green known as *yu choy* provides a wonderful contrast to the sweet curry sauce. Now there's a meal that will impress your friends.

Creative, delicious, doable, foolproof…welcome to the flavors of your new favorite cookbook.

Goat Cheese and Black Pepper Biscuits
with Smoked Salmon and Dill (page 11)

Starters

Appetizers

Soups

Beverages

Caponata with Fennel, Olives, and Raisins

6 tablespoons olive oil

1½ pounds unpeeled eggplant, cut into ¾-inch cubes

3 cups chopped red bell peppers

2 cups chopped fresh fennel

6 large garlic cloves, chopped

½ cup pitted Kalamata olives, chopped

½ cup golden raisins

1¼ cups tomato sauce

6 tablespoons red wine vinegar

¾ cup chopped fresh basil

Toasted baguette slices

Heat olive oil in large pot over medium-high heat. Add eggplant, bell peppers, fennel, and garlic; sauté 10 minutes. Add chopped olives and raisins, then mix in tomato sauce and red wine vinegar. Cover, reduce heat to medium-low, and simmer 15 minutes, stirring occasionally. Uncover and simmer until caponata is thick and vegetables are tender, stirring often, about 15 minutes. Mix in basil. Season caponata to taste with salt and pepper. (*Can be made 1 day ahead. Cover and chill.*) Serve at room temperature with baguette slices.

MAKES 6 CUPS

Goat Cheese and Black Pepper Biscuits with Smoked Salmon and Dill

     2 cups all purpose flour
     2 teaspoons baking powder
     1 teaspoon sugar
    ½ teaspoon baking soda
    ½ teaspoon salt
    ½ teaspoon freshly ground black pepper
    ¼ cup (½ stick) chilled butter, cut into ½-inch cubes
     1 5-ounce log soft fresh goat cheese, crumbled
    ¾ cup buttermilk

        European-style butter (such as Plugrá), room temperature
     6 ounces thinly sliced smoked salmon
     1 large bunch fresh dill sprigs

Preheat oven to 400°F. Line 2 heavy large baking sheets with parchment paper. Whisk first 6 ingredients in large bowl. Using fingertips, rub butter into dry ingredients until coarse meal forms. Add cheese and buttermilk; stir with fork just until dough comes together (bits of cheese will be visible in dough).

Pat dough out on lightly floured surface into ¾-inch-thick round. Using floured 2-inch-diameter cutter, cut out biscuits. Gather scraps and pat dough out; cut out additional biscuits. Arrange on prepared baking sheets and bake 6 minutes. Turn sheets; bake until golden brown, about 8 minutes longer. Cool biscuits on rack. (*Biscuits can be made 6 hours ahead. Let stand at room temperature.*)

Split biscuits in half horizontally. Spread bottom halves with thin layer of butter. Divide salmon among biscuits. Top each with dill sprig and biscuit top.

MAKES ABOUT 16

Italian Dinner for 8

Caponata with Fennel, Olives, and Raisins
(*opposite; pictured opposite*)

Veal Chops with Roasted Tomatoes, Arugula, and Soft Polenta
(*double recipe; page 48*)

Tricolore Salad

Sangiovese

Hazelnut Tozzetti
(*page 231*)

Assorted Chocolates

Vin Santo

Seared Sea Scallops with Banyuls Vinegar and Chicory Slaw

²/₃ cup plus 2 tablespoons extra-virgin olive oil

6 tablespoons Banyuls vinegar or Sherry wine vinegar, divided

1 shallot, thinly slivered

12 ounces assorted red and green chicories (such as radicchio, red and green Belgian endive, escarole hearts, and frisée)

24 large sea scallops

3 tablespoons water

Whisk ²/₃ cup oil, 3 tablespoons vinegar, and shallot in small bowl to blend. Season vinaigrette to taste with salt and pepper.

Very thinly slice radicchio and endive; tear escarole and frisée into 2-inch lengths. Place in large bowl. (*Vinaigrette and slaw can be made 6 hours ahead. Chill dressing; let stand at room temperature 30 minutes before using. Place damp kitchen towel over slaw and chill.*)

Heat 2 tablespoons oil in large nonstick skillet over medium-high heat. Sprinkle scallops with salt and pepper. Working in batches, add scallops to skillet and cook until golden and just opaque in center, about 1½ minutes per side.

Rewhisk vinaigrette; pour over slaw and toss to coat. Divide slaw among 8 plates. Arrange 3 scallops atop slaw on each plate. Add remaining 3 tablespoons vinegar to same skillet along with 3 tablespoons water. Bring to boil over medium heat, scraping up any browned bits and dissolving any caramelized juices. Drizzle juices over scallops and serve.

8 SERVINGS

Banyuls vinegar is a rich, oak-aged vinegar (made from the naturally sweet wine of the same name) from the south of France. It can be found at specialty foods stores.

Soy-Sake Shrimp with Ginger Aioli

½ cup soy sauce
2 green onions, chopped
6 tablespoons olive oil, divided
2 tablespoons unseasoned rice vinegar
2 tablespoons sake or dry Sherry
1 tablespoon golden brown sugar
3 garlic cloves, chopped
24 deveined peeled uncooked large shrimp (about 1½ pounds)

1 cup mayonnaise
1 tablespoon chopped peeled fresh ginger

Cooked white rice

This twist on the classic garlic mayonnaise is as simple as blending mayo and fresh ginger in a processor.

Combine soy sauce, green onions, 4 tablespoons oil, vinegar, sake, brown sugar, and garlic in 13x9x2-inch glass baking dish; whisk marinade to blend. Add shrimp and toss to coat. Refrigerate at least 30 minutes and up to 1 hour, turning shrimp occasionally.

Blend mayonnaise and ginger in food processor until smooth. Transfer ginger aioli to small bowl and refrigerate.

Drain marinade from shrimp into small saucepan; bring to boil. Whisk 2 tablespoons boiled marinade into ginger aioli; reserve remaining boiled marinade.

Heat remaining 2 tablespoons oil in heavy large skillet over medium-high heat. Add shrimp; sauté until just opaque in center, about 4 minutes. Mound rice in center of plates. Arrange shrimp around rice; drizzle with ginger aioli. Serve, passing reserved boiled marinade.

6 SERVINGS

Chicken Satays on Lemongrass Spears with Peanut Sauce

PEANUT SAUCE

- 1 cup old-fashioned (all natural) smooth peanut butter
- ½ cup low-salt chicken broth
- ¼ cup unseasoned rice vinegar
- 3 tablespoons palm sugar* or dark brown sugar
- 2 tablespoons tamari soy sauce*
- 2 tablespoons minced fresh ginger
- 2 teaspoons hot chili sauce or paste (such as sambal oelek or sriracha)*
- 1 teaspoon turmeric

CHICKEN

- 1½ cups sliced shallots (about 10)
- ½ cup shredded dried unsweetened coconut
- ½ cup chopped fresh cilantro
- 6 garlic cloves, peeled
- 3 double-leaf kaffir lime leaves,* thinly sliced
- 2 serrano chiles, stemmed
- 1 1-inch cube peeled galangal* or fresh ginger, chopped
- 2 tablespoons vegetable oil
- 2 pounds boneless chicken thighs with skin, cut into 1-inch pieces
- 1 teaspoon salt

- 16 whole lemongrass stalks*

     Nonstick vegetable oil spray

FOR PEANUT SAUCE: Stir all ingredients in small saucepan over medium heat until thickened, about 2 minutes. Season with salt and pepper. Transfer to small bowl. (*Can be made 3 days ahead. Cover; chill. Microwave on low setting until lukewarm and stir well before serving.*)

FOR CHICKEN: Grind first 7 ingredients in processor to coarse paste. Heat oil in medium skillet over medium heat. Add paste to skillet; do not clean processor. Sauté paste until just brown, about 5 minutes; transfer to large bowl and cool. Add chicken and salt to processor; grind coarsely. Mix chicken into paste in bowl.

Press ¼ cup chicken mixture around thick portion of 1 lemongrass stalk in 4-inch-long sausage shape, leaving 1 inch of stalk exposed. Repeat with remaining chicken mixture and stalks. (*Can be made 1 day ahead. Place on plastic-lined baking sheet, cover, and chill.*)

Spray grill with nonstick spray and prepare barbecue (medium-high heat). Grill satays until chicken is cooked through, turning often, about 8 minutes. Serve with warm peanut sauce.

Available in the Asian foods section of supermarkets, at specialty foods stores, and at Asian markets.

MAKES 16

Spicy Shrimp Remoulade on Molasses-Buttered Toasts

MOLASSES BUTTER

6 tablespoons (¾ stick) butter, room temperature

2 teaspoons light molasses

¼ teaspoon chili powder

REMOULADE SAUCE

½ cup mayonnaise

3 tablespoons finely chopped celery

1½ tablespoons chopped Italian parsley

2½ teaspoons drained prepared white horseradish

2 teaspoons minced shallot

2 teaspoons ketchup

2 teaspoons whole grain Dijon mustard

1 teaspoon grated lemon peel

1 teaspoon Worcestershire sauce

1 teaspoon paprika

1 small garlic clove, minced

¼ teaspoon cayenne pepper

24 1½-inch rounds or squares cut from Westphalian-style pumpernickel bread slices

8 ounces cooked peeled medium shrimp, cut into ½-inch pieces

2 tablespoons chopped fresh chives

FOR MOLASSES BUTTER: Using fork, mix all ingredients in small bowl to blend.

FOR REMOULADE SAUCE: Mix first 12 ingredients in medium bowl.

Preheat oven to 425°F. Spread molasses butter lightly over bread; arrange in single layer on baking sheet. Bake until bread begins to firm up, about 10 minutes. Cool.

Mix shrimp into remoulade sauce. Top toasts with shrimp mixture. Sprinkle with chives. Place toasts on platter.

8 SERVINGS

Chilled shrimp in piquant remoulade sauce is a Creole classic. Here, it tops pumpernickel toasts spread with a chili-molasses butter.

Artichoke-Olive "Chips and Dip"

Steamed artichoke leaves are the perfect chips to dip into a citrusy artichoke-olive sauté.

8 large fresh artichokes, stems trimmed

¼ cup olive oil

½ cup chopped leek (white and pale green parts only)

6 garlic cloves, minced

2 tablespoons (¼ stick) butter

3 tablespoons chopped pitted Kalamata olives

3 tablespoons chopped fresh parsley

2 tablespoons fresh lemon juice

1 teaspoon chopped fresh thyme

½ teaspoon grated lemon peel

¼ teaspoon dried crushed red pepper

Add water to depth of 2 inches in 2 large pots; bring to boil. Add salt to water, then divide artichokes between pots. Bring to boil; cover. Reduce heat to medium, simmer until artichokes are just tender when pierced in base, about 25 minutes. Transfer artichokes to plates to cool.

Working with 1 artichoke at a time, break off large outer leaves and reserve. Discard smaller leaves near heart. Using spoon, scoop out choke. Chop heart into ¼-inch cubes; place in large bowl.

Heat oil in large skillet over medium-low heat. Add leek and garlic; sauté until tender, about 5 minutes. Add butter; stir until melted. Add chopped artichokes, olives, parsley, lemon juice, thyme, lemon peel, and red pepper. Simmer 5 minutes, stirring often. Cool. (Can be made 1 day ahead. Cover artichoke heart mixture and leaves separately; chill.)

Transfer chopped artichoke mixture to center of large shallow bowl or platter. Place artichoke leaves around artichoke mixture and serve.

MAKES ABOUT 2½ CUPS

Crostini with Fresh Mozzarella and Anchovy Sauce

2 tablespoons (¼ stick) unsalted butter
2 anchovy fillets, drained, chopped
1 tablespoon whole milk

18 ½-inch-thick slices crusty bread or baguette
2 tablespoons extra-virgin olive oil
½ pound fresh buffalo mozzarella cheese, thinly sliced, patted dry

Preheat broiler. Combine butter, anchovies, and milk in small saucepan over low heat. Cook until anchovies dissolve, mashing with back of spoon and stirring often, about 3 minutes (do not boil).

Place bread slices on rimmed baking sheet. Brush with oil; top with mozzarella slices. Broil until cheese melts and bread crisps, watching closely to prevent burning, about 3 minutes. Transfer crostini to platter.

Drizzle sauce over crostini and serve.

MAKES 18

Minted Sugar Snap and Lima Bean Dip with Toasted Pita

1 pound sugar snap peas
¾ cup frozen baby lima beans or frozen shelled edamame, thawed
½ cup olive oil, plus additional oil for pitas
½ cup fresh mint leaves
2 teaspoons fresh lemon juice
Pinch of sugar

6 7-inch-diameter pita breads

Cook peas in saucepan of boiling salted water until tender, about 3 minutes. Using slotted spoon, transfer peas to processor. Add lima beans to same pan of boiling water; cook until tender, about 8 minutes. Drain lima beans; add to processor. Add ½ cup olive oil, mint leaves, lemon juice, and sugar. Puree until smooth. Season dip to taste with salt and pepper. Transfer to serving bowl.

Preheat oven to 350°F. Brush each pita on both sides with olive oil; cut each into 8 triangles. Arrange triangles on rimmed baking sheets. Bake until light golden, about 12 minutes. Cool completely on sheets. (*Can be made 4 hours ahead. Chill dip; cover pitas and store at room temperature.*) Arrange pitas on platter with dip.

6 SERVINGS

Honeydew and Prosciutto with Greens and Mint Vinaigrette

1 tablespoon Sherry wine vinegar
1 teaspoon honey
¼ teaspoon aniseed
3 tablespoons thinly sliced fresh mint, divided
2 tablespoons olive oil
4 cups (packed) mixed baby greens (about 3 ounces)
4 honeydew melon wedges, peeled
6 thin slices prosciutto

Whisk first 3 ingredients and 1 tablespoon mint in small bowl; whisk in oil. Season dressing to taste with salt and pepper. Toss greens with 2 tablespoons dressing in medium bowl; divide between 2 plates. Place melon next to greens; drape prosciutto over melon. Drizzle remaining dressing over prosciutto and melon. Sprinkle with remaining 2 tablespoons mint and freshly ground pepper and serve.

2 SERVINGS

Lunch on the Patio for 6

Minted Sugar Snap and
Lima Bean Dip with
Toasted Pita
(opposite)

Oven-Dried Tomato Tart with
Goat Cheese and Black Olives
(page 112)

Mixed Green Salad

Sauvignon Blanc and *Iced Tea*

Apricot-Raspberry Pavlovas
with Sliced Almonds
(page 193)

Onion and Bacon Tart

    8 bacon slices, chopped
    5 cups sliced onions (about 3 large)

    1 large egg
  ½ cup sour cream
    1 teaspoon salt
  ½ teaspoon ground black pepper
      Pinch of ground nutmeg

    1 13.8-ounce tube refrigerated pizza dough
  ¼ teaspoon caraway seeds

Preheat oven to 375°F. Sauté bacon in heavy large skillet over medium-high heat until slightly crisp. Drain all but 1 tablespoon bacon drippings from skillet. Add onions to bacon and sauté over medium heat until onions are very tender but not brown, about 20 minutes. Cool.

Whisk egg, sour cream, salt, pepper, and nutmeg in large bowl to blend. Stir in cooled onion mixture.

Roll pizza dough out on lightly floured surface to 13x10-inch rectangle. Transfer to baking sheet. Spread onion mixture over dough, leaving ½-inch plain border around edges. Sprinkle with caraway seeds.

Bake tart until onion custard is set and crust is golden brown around edges and brown on bottom, about 25 minutes.

6 SERVINGS

Roasted Red Pepper and Feta Dip

    4 red bell peppers
  ¼ cup extra-virgin olive oil
    2 garlic cloves, peeled
    2 cups crumbled feta cheese

Char peppers directly over gas flame or in broiler until blackened on all sides. Enclose in paper bag 10 minutes. Peel, seed, and quarter peppers. Puree peppers, oil, garlic, and cheese in processor. Season with salt and pepper. Chill at least 3 hours or overnight.

MAKES ABOUT 3½ CUPS

Saffron Chicken Broth with Spinach Matzo Balls

SAFFRON CHICKEN BROTH

- 6 pounds chicken wings
- 16 cups water
- 1½ pounds onions, quartered
- 6 bay leaves
- 1 tablespoon coarse kosher salt
- 1½ teaspoons saffron threads

SPINACH MATZO BALLS

- 4 large eggs
- 1¼ teaspoons coarse kosher salt
- ½ teaspoon ground black pepper
- 1 cup unsalted matzo meal
- 1 10-ounce package frozen chopped spinach, thawed, squeezed dry

FOR SAFFRON CHICKEN BROTH: Bring all ingredients to boil in very large pot. Reduce heat to medium-low, partially cover, and simmer 2 hours, stirring occasionally. Strain broth into another pot. Spoon ¼ cup fat from top of broth and place in medium bowl; add ¼ cup broth. Cool fat mixture and reserve for matzo balls. Remove enough meat from chicken wings to measure 1 generous cup. Finely mince chicken; reserve for matzo balls. Chill remaining broth until ready to use. (*Can be made 2 days ahead. Cover and keep chilled.*)

FOR SPINACH MATZO BALLS: Whisk eggs, salt, and pepper into chicken fat mixture. Mix in matzo meal, then spinach and reserved minced chicken. Cover and chill until firm, at least 1 hour and up to 1 day.

Bring large pot of generously salted water to boil. Using wet hands and about 2 tablespoons for each, shape matzo mixture into 16 balls; drop into boiling water. Reduce heat to low, cover pot, and simmer until tender, about 45 minutes. Using slotted spoon, transfer matzo balls to 13x9x2-inch dish. (*Can be made 1 day ahead; chill.*)

Skim any fat from top of broth; bring to simmer. Season with salt and pepper. Add cooked matzo balls; simmer until heated through, about 10 minutes.

Ladle broth and matzo balls into bowls and serve.

8 SERVINGS

SOUPS

Speedy Gazpacho

1 English hothouse cucumber (about 12 ounces), peeled, cut into large chunks

1 large red bell pepper (about 8 ounces), halved, seeded, cut into chunks

2 cups (or more) bottled tomato juice

1 14½-ounce can diced tomatoes in juice

1 12½-ounce container refrigerated fire-roasted tomato salsa

1 cup roasted red peppers from jar

½ cup coarsely chopped fresh cilantro

2 tablespoons red wine vinegar

Diced avocado (optional)

Steamed shrimp (optional)

Working in 2 batches and using on/off turns, finely chop cucumber and bell pepper in processor. Add 2 cups tomato juice and remaining ingredients; blend to coarse puree. Season to taste with salt. Transfer to bowl. Cover and chill 2 hours for flavors to develop. Mix in more tomato juice by ¼ cupfuls if too spicy. Serve, garnishing with avocado and shrimp, if desired.

6 TO 8 SERVINGS

Chilled Zucchini-Mint Soup

1 tablespoon butter

⅓ cup extra-virgin olive oil

5 cups chopped leeks (white and pale green parts only; about 6 leeks)

3 pounds zucchini, trimmed, chopped (about 8 cups)

5½ cups (or more) vegetable broth

⅓ cup whipping cream

1½ tablespoons (packed) minced fresh mint plus whole leaves for garnish

Melt butter with oil in heavy large pot over medium-high heat. Add leeks and sauté until soft but not brown, about 5 minutes. Add zucchini and sauté until beginning to soften, about 5 minutes. Add 5½ cups broth and bring to boil. Reduce heat to medium-low.

Simmer uncovered until zucchini is very tender, about 20 minutes. Working in batches, puree soup in blender until smooth. Return puree to same pot. Mix in cream and minced mint. Cover and chill until cold, at least 3 hours and up to 1 day.

Thin soup with more broth if too thick. Season with salt and pepper. Ladle into bowls. Garnish with mint leaves.

8 SERVINGS

Mulligatawny Soup

¼ cup vegetable oil
3 cups chopped onions (about 1 pound)
5 garlic cloves, chopped
1½ tablespoons garam masala
1½ teaspoons ground coriander
1 teaspoon turmeric
½ teaspoon cayenne pepper
2 bay leaves
2 cups dried red lentils
8 cups low-salt chicken broth

2 cups diced cooked chicken
1 cup canned unsweetened coconut milk
3 tablespoons fresh lemon juice

2 cups cooked basmati rice
Lemon wedges

Heat vegetable oil in heavy large pot over medium-high heat. Add onions and cook until golden brown, stirring frequently, about 15 minutes. Add garlic and sauté 2 minutes. Add garam masala and next 4 ingredients; stir 1 minute. Add lentils; stir until coated. Add chicken broth. Bring soup to boil; reduce heat to medium and simmer until lentils are very tender, about 20 minutes. Discard bay leaves.

Working in batches, puree soup in blender until smooth. Return to pot. Stir in chicken, coconut milk, and lemon juice. Season to taste with salt and pepper.

Divide rice among bowls. Pour soup over. Garnish with lemon wedges and serve.

8 SERVINGS

**Summer Supper
Under the Stars for 8**

Chilled Zucchini-Mint Soup
(opposite)

Chicken with Tangerine, Honey,
and Chipotle Glaze
(double recipe; page 68)

Corn on the Cob with
Lime-Chive Butter
(page 138)

Caesar Salad

Chardonnay

Berries in
Sweet Fragolino Wine
with Biscotti
(page 189)

Roasted Beet Soup with Crème Fraîche

½	pound red beets (about 3 medium)
1½	teaspoons butter
1½	teaspoons olive oil
1	leek (white and pale green parts only), chopped
1	small onion, thinly sliced
1	celery stalk, chopped
⅛	teaspoon ground ginger
⅛	teaspoon ground allspice
⅛	teaspoon ground white pepper
2	cups water
1	small bay leaf
1	fresh thyme sprig
1	fresh parsley sprig
¼	cup whipping cream
2	tablespoons crème fraîche or sour cream

Preheat oven to 350°F. Wrap beets in foil and roast until tender when pierced with fork, about 1 hour. Cool. Peel beets. Cut ¼ of 1 beet into ¼-inch cubes; reserve for garnish. Cut remaining beets into ½-inch pieces.

Melt butter with oil in heavy medium saucepan over medium-high heat. Add leek, onion, and celery and cook until beginning to brown, stirring often, about 13 minutes. Stir in ginger, allspice, white pepper, and ½-inch beet pieces. Cook until vegetables begin to stick to bottom of pot, stirring often, about 7 minutes. Add 2 cups water, bay leaf, thyme sprig, and parsley sprig. Bring to boil. Reduce heat to low, cover, and simmer until vegetables are very tender, about 25 minutes. Remove bay leaf, thyme sprig, and parsley sprig. Cool soup slightly. Working in batches, puree in blender with cream. Season with salt and pepper. *(Can be made 1 day ahead. Cool slightly, cover, and chill.)*

Gently rewarm soup (do not boil). Ladle into 2 bowls. Garnish each with 1 tablespoon crème fraîche. Sprinkle with reserved beet cubes.

2 SERVINGS

Pair the soup with a light red wine, like an Oregon Pinot Noir.

Fennel-Saffron Soup with Poached Oysters

 2 tablespoons (¼ stick) unsalted butter
 2 medium fennel bulbs, trimmed, each cut lengthwise into 6 wedges
 1 cup water

 1 tablespoon olive oil
 3 garlic cloves, chopped
 ⅛ teaspoon crumbled saffron threads
 4 8-ounce bottles clam juice
 1 cup whipping cream
 3 tablespoons Pernod or other anise-flavored liqueur
 3 cups freshly shucked oysters or three 8-ounce jars
   shucked oysters

Melt butter in heavy medium skillet over medium heat. Add fennel and sauté until golden, about 10 minutes. Add 1 cup water; cover and cook until fennel is very tender, about 20 minutes. Puree fennel mixture in processor. Set aside.

Heat oil in heavy large saucepan over medium heat. Add garlic and saffron; sauté 1 minute. Add clam juice, cream, and Pernod and bring to simmer. Add fennel puree and bring to simmer. *(Can be made 1 day ahead. Refrigerate uncovered until cold. Cover and keep refrigerated. Simmer before continuing.)* Add oysters with their liquor to cream mixture and stir to heat through. Ladle soup into bowls.

8 SERVINGS

Barley and Lentil Soup with Swiss Chard

1 tablespoon olive oil

1½ cups chopped onions

1½ cups chopped peeled carrots

3 large garlic cloves, minced

2½ teaspoons ground cumin

10 cups (or more) low-salt chicken or vegetable broth

⅔ cup pearl barley

1 14½-ounce can diced tomatoes in juice

⅔ cup dried lentils

4 cups (packed) coarsely chopped Swiss chard (about ½ large bunch)

2 tablespoons chopped fresh dill

Heat oil in heavy large nonreactive pot over medium-high heat. Add onions and carrots; sauté until onions are golden brown, about 10 minutes. Add garlic and stir 1 minute. Mix in cumin; stir 30 seconds. Add 10 cups broth and barley; bring to boil. Reduce heat; partially cover and simmer 25 minutes. Stir in tomatoes with juice and lentils; cover and simmer until barley and lentils are tender, about 30 minutes.

Add chard to soup; cover and simmer until chard is tender, about 5 minutes. Stir in dill. Season soup with salt and pepper. Thin with more broth, if desired.

10 SERVINGS

Chilled Corn Soup with Adobo Swirl

3 tablespoons olive oil, divided
1 cup chopped sweet onion (such as Vidalia or Maui)
3 cups fresh corn kernels (cut from about 3 ears of corn)
2 cups low-salt chicken broth
2 tablespoons fresh lime juice, divided
1 cup (or more) water

1 teaspoon adobo sauce from canned chipotle chiles
   Fresh cilantro leaves

Adobo is the spicy tomato sauce that comes in the can with chipotle chiles. Canned chipotles are available at supermarkets, specialty foods stores, and Latin markets.

Heat 1 tablespoon olive oil in heavy large saucepan over medium-high heat. Add onion and sauté until soft, about 4 minutes. Add corn kernels, broth, and 1 tablespoon lime juice; bring mixture to boil. Reduce heat to medium and simmer until corn is just tender, about 3 minutes. Working in batches, puree soup in blender until almost smooth. Stir in remaining 1 tablespoon lime juice and 1 cup water (or more as needed to thin soup to desired consistency). Season corn soup to taste with salt and pepper. Transfer soup to large bowl; cover and refrigerate until chilled, about 2 hours or overnight.

Meanwhile, whisk remaining 2 tablespoons olive oil and adobo sauce in small bowl to blend. Divide chilled corn soup among 4 bowls. Drizzle soup with adobo oil, then garnish with cilantro and serve.

4 SERVINGS

Carrot Soup with Orange and Tarragon

    1 tablespoon butter
    1 1-pound bag classic-cut peeled carrots
    ¾ cup chopped onion
    3 cups low-salt chicken broth

    ½ cup orange juice
    1 tablespoon brandy
    2 teaspoons chopped fresh tarragon
       Fresh tarragon sprigs

Melt butter in heavy large pot over medium heat. Add carrots and onion; sauté until onion is soft, about 8 minutes. Add broth; cover and bring to boil. Reduce heat, uncover, and simmer until carrots are tender, about 10 minutes.

Working in batches, puree soup in blender until very smooth. Return soup to pot. Stir in orange juice, brandy, and chopped tarragon. Simmer 5 minutes for flavors to blend. Season to taste with salt and pepper. Garnish soup with tarragon sprigs and serve.

4 SERVINGS

Broccoli Soup with Chive-Cayenne Oil

    ¼ cup plus 1 tablespoon extra-virgin olive oil
    ¼ cup coarsely chopped chives
       Pinch of cayenne pepper

    1 medium onion, chopped
    1 fresh or 2 dried Turkish bay leaves
    1 pound broccoli, stems and crowns cut into 1-inch pieces (about 6 cups)
    4 cups low-salt chicken broth

Puree ¼ cup oil, chives, and cayenne in blender. Season with salt. Set aside.

Heat 1 tablespoon oil in large saucepan over medium-high heat. Add onion and bay leaves; cook until onion is golden, stirring often, about 7 minutes. Add broccoli; stir until bright green, about 1 minute. Add broth. Simmer until broccoli is tender, about 5 minutes. Remove bay leaves. Cool soup slightly.

Working in batches, puree soup in blender until smooth, about 1 minute per batch. Return soup to pot. Rewarm until hot. Season to taste with salt and pepper.

Divide soup among 6 bowls. Drizzle with chive-cayenne oil and serve.

6 SERVINGS

Strawberry and Peach Sangria

 1 750-ml bottle dry white wine
1¾ cups Essensia (orange Muscat, a sweet dessert wine)
1¾ cups sliced strawberries
 1 cup peach liqueur
 3 peaches, each cut into 12 slices
 1 large orange, cut crosswise into 6 slices
 1 large lemon, cut crosswise into 6 slices
 ¼ cup strawberry syrup (optional)
 3 to 4 cups ice cubes

BEVERAGES

Mix white wine, Essensia, strawberries, peach liqueur, peaches, orange slices, lemon slices, and strawberry syrup (if using) in large pitcher, smashing citrus slices slightly. Let stand at room temperature at least 2 hours or chill up to 4 hours. Serve sangria over ice.

8 SERVINGS

Frozen Watermelon Daiquiris

4 strawberries, halved, plus ¾ cup sliced strawberries
1 kiwi, peeled, cut into 8 wedges
4 4-inch-long lemongrass skewers

5 tablespoons light rum
3 tablespoons sour watermelon liqueur (such as Pucker)*
2 tablespoons sugar
2 tablespoons fresh lime juice
3 cups ¾-inch cubes seedless watermelon, frozen at least 1 hour

Thread strawberry halves and kiwi wedges alternately onto lemongrass skewers.

Stir light rum, sour watermelon liqueur, sugar, and fresh lime juice in small bowl until sugar dissolves. Transfer mixture to blender. Add frozen watermelon cubes and ¾ cup sliced strawberries. Blend mixture well; pour into Martini glasses. Garnish with lemongrass skewers.

Available at some supermarkets and many liquor stores.

MAKES 4

Strawberries and kiwi wedges are threaded onto lemongrass skewers for a fun garnish. To make the skewers, cut a four-inch piece from the tough end of a lemongrass stalk, then peel away the outer layers until only a ¼-inch-diameter skewer remains. Look for lemongrass in the produce section of some supermarkets and also at Asian markets.

Mulled Cranberry, Apple, and Rum Cider

1 large orange
3 cups cranberry juice cocktail
3 cups apple cider
¾ cup (packed) golden brown sugar
4¾ 3- to 4-inch-long cinnamon sticks
18 whole cloves
¾ teaspoon ground nutmeg
6 tablespoons dark rum
6 additional 3- to 4-inch-long cinnamon sticks (optional)
6 orange slices (optional)

Using vegetable peeler, remove peel from orange in long strips. Place strips in large saucepan; halve orange and squeeze juice into pan. Add cranberry juice cocktail, cider, sugar, 4¾ cinnamon sticks, cloves, and nutmeg. Bring to boil over high heat, stirring until sugar dissolves. Reduce heat to medium and simmer 25 minutes. (*Can be made 1 day ahead. Cover and chill.*) Add rum to cider; simmer 5 minutes. Ladle into mugs. Garnish with cinnamon sticks and orange slices, if desired.

MAKES ABOUT 6 CUPS

Citrus-Blossom Gin Fizz

CITRUS-BLOSSOM SYRUP

- 2 cups water
- 2 cups sugar
- 1 tablespoon loosely packed fresh lemon verbena leaves (optional)
- 1 orange
- 1 lemon
- 2 teaspoons orange-flower water*

DRINKS

- 6 cups ice cubes, divided
- ¾ cup gin, divided
- ¾ cup whipping cream, divided
- 4 large egg whites, divided
- 4 tablespoons lemon juice, divided
- Freshly ground nutmeg
- Fresh lemon verbena sprigs (optional)

The citrus-scented sugar syrup will make more than enough for eight drinks. Use the extra syrup for seconds, or save it for sweetening other citrus cocktails.

FOR CITRUS BLOSSOM SYRUP: Mix 2 cups water, sugar, and lemon verbena, if desired, in medium saucepan. Using vegetable peeler, remove peel (colored part) from orange and lemon; add peel to saucepan. Bring sugar mixture to boil, stirring until sugar dissolves. Reduce heat to medium and simmer 5 minutes. Cool completely. Stir in orange-flower water. (*Can be made 2 weeks ahead. Cover and refrigerate.*)

FOR DRINKS: Combine 6 tablespoons syrup, 3 cups ice, ¼ cup gin, ¼ cup cream, 2 egg whites, and 2 tablespoons lemon juice in blender. Blend until smooth and foamy. Divide among 4 glasses. Repeat with 6 tablespoons syrup and remaining ice, gin, cream, egg whites, and juice. Sprinkle with nutmeg; garnish with lemon verbena sprigs, if desired.

A flavoring extract; available in the liquor aisle or baking section of some supermarkets and at liquor stores and Middle Eastern markets.

8 SERVINGS

Berry Rum Punch

⅔ cup water
⅔ cup sugar
3 cups fresh raspberries, divided

2 cups fresh orange juice
2 cups pineapple juice
1 cup dark rum
1 cup light rum
1 orange, peeled, diced
1 cup diced peeled fresh pineapple
¾ teaspoon vanilla extract
Ice cubes

Orange slices

Bring ⅔ cup water and sugar to boil in medium saucepan, stirring until sugar dissolves. Remove from heat; cool syrup completely. Puree 2 cups raspberries in processor. Pour puree through fine strainer set over saucepan with syrup. Press on solids to extract as much liquid as possible; discard solids.

Mix orange juice, next 6 ingredients, 1 cup berries, and raspberry syrup in glass bowl. Cover; refrigerate at least 4 hours and up to 1 day. Strain into pitcher. Serve punch over ice. Garnish with orange slices.

8 SERVINGS

Rose Royale

8 candied rose petals
3 teaspoons vodka
1⅓ cups chilled rosé Champagne

Divide rose petals between Champagne flutes. Add 1½ teaspoons vodka to each, then ⅔ cup chilled Champagne to each and serve.

MAKES 2

Bull Shot

¾ teaspoon Worcestershire sauce
⅛ teaspoon celery salt
  Ice cubes
¼ cup vodka
¾ cup chilled double-rich double-strength canned beef broth
  Lime wedge

Mix Worcestershire and salt in glass. Add ice cubes. Pour vodka, then broth over. Garnish with lime wedge.

MAKES 1

Think of this drink as a Bloody Mary made with broth instead of tomato juice.

Anno 1960

  Ice
3 tablespoons vodka
1½ tablespoons dry vermouth
1½ tablespoons Campari

Fill cocktail shaker with ice. Add 3 tablespoons vodka, 1½ tablespoons dry vermouth, and 1½ tablespoons Campari; shake well. Strain into a Martini glass.

MAKES 1

This little-known classic Italian cocktail is a leaner, crisper spin on the Negroni.

Passion Fruit-Pineapple Vodka Coolers

3 cups premium vodka
1½ cups thawed frozen passion fruit juice concentrate
¾ cup thawed frozen pineapple juice concentrate
¾ cup fresh lime juice
1 tablespoon blue curacao liqueur
8 ripe passion fruits
1 quart club soda
  Ice

Combine first 5 ingredients in large pitcher. Scoop out the fruit (with seeds) from passion fruits. Add to pitcher and stir to blend. Mix in club soda. Pour into glasses filled with ice.

MAKES 8

Brown Sugar and Bourbon Ribs (page 59)

Main Courses

Meats

Poultry

Seafood

Meatless

Pasta & Pizza

Grilled Steak Sandwiches with Chimichurri and Bell Peppers

1 cup (packed) fresh Italian parsley
1 cup (packed) fresh cilantro
3 tablespoons white wine vinegar
2 tablespoons chopped fresh oregano
2 garlic cloves, peeled
½ teaspoon dried crushed red pepper
⅔ cup plus ¼ cup olive oil

2 large bell peppers (preferably 1 red and 1 yellow), cut into ¾-inch-wide strips
2 12-ounce rib-eye steaks
4 sourdough demi-baguettes, halved horizontally

Prepare barbecue (medium-high heat). Combine first 6 ingredients in processor; add ⅔ cup oil and puree until almost smooth. Season chimichurri with salt and pepper.

Brush pepper strips, steaks, and cut side of bread with remaining ¼ cup oil. Sprinkle peppers and steaks with salt and pepper. Grill peppers until tender, about 5 minutes per side. Grill steaks to desired doneness, about 4 minutes per side for medium-rare. Grill bread, cut side down, until beginning to brown lightly, about 2 minutes. Thinly slice steaks crosswise; divide among bread bottoms. Spoon chimichurri over steak (about ¼ cup per sandwich), then top with pepper strips. Cover with bread tops and serve.

4 SERVINGS

Chimichurri is an Argentine parsley sauce with bright flavors and a kick from crushed red pepper. To save time: Prepare the fresh parsley and cilantro for the processor by simply cutting off the tops of the bunches and discarding the bottom stems.

Steak Chinois

7	tablespoons canola oil, divided
¼	cup plus 1 tablespoon tamari sauce or soy sauce
3	tablespoons plus 1 teaspoon finely grated peeled fresh ginger
2	garlic cloves, chopped
1	1½-pound flank steak
1¼	cups whipping cream
4	tablespoons sliced green onions, divided

A tamari-ginger marinade and sauce gives the seared flank steak an Asian twist.

Mix 6 tablespoons oil, ¼ cup tamari, 3 tablespoons ginger, and garlic in 13x9x2-inch glass dish. Add steak, turning to coat. Cover and refrigerate overnight.

Remove steak from marinade; pat dry. Heat 1 tablespoon oil in large skillet over high heat. Add steak; cook until browned, about 4 minutes per side for medium-rare. Transfer steak to platter. Reduce heat to medium-high. Add cream and 2 tablespoons green onions to skillet; bring to boil, scraping up browned bits. Add 1 tablespoon tamari and 1 teaspoon ginger; boil to sauce consistency, about 3 minutes. Season sauce with pepper.

Cut steak across grain on diagonal into ¼-inch-thick slices. Divide steak among 4 plates. Drizzle with sauce and sprinkle with 2 tablespoons green onions.

4 SERVINGS

Roasted Vegetable Meatloaf
with Mustard Mashed Potatoes

  3 small zucchini, diced
  3 red bell peppers, diced
  2 medium-size red onions, diced
  2 tablespoons olive oil
  2 tablespoons chopped fresh rosemary, divided

  2 pounds ground beef chuck (20% fat)
  2 cups coarsely grated whole-milk mozzarella cheese (about 8 ounces)
1½ cups panko (Japanese breadcrumbs)
  1 cup thinly sliced fresh basil
  1 tablespoon chopped fresh marjoram
1½ teaspoons salt

½ teaspoon ground black pepper
½ teaspoon dried crushed red pepper
1 cup ketchup, divided
2 large eggs
¼ cup dry red wine
Mustard Mashed Potatoes (see recipe)

Preheat oven to 450°F. Combine zucchini, peppers, and onions in medium bowl. Add oil and 1 tablespoon rosemary; toss to coat. Spread evenly on rimmed baking sheet; sprinkle with salt and pepper. Roast until tender, about 25 minutes. Remove from oven; cool.

Preheat oven to 375°F. Mix ground beef, mozzarella, panko, basil, marjoram, 1½ teaspoons salt, ½ teaspoon pepper, dried crushed pepper, 1 tablespoon rosemary, and 1 cup roasted vegetables in large bowl. Whisk ½ cup ketchup, eggs, and wine in medium bowl. Add to beef mixture; stir with wooden spoon until well incorporated. Spoon into 9x5x3-inch loaf pan, forming rounded top.

Spoon ½ cup ketchup over top of loaf. Bake meatloaf until cooked through, juices run clear, and top is browned, about 1 hour 10 minutes. Remove pan from oven; let meatloaf rest 20 minutes.

Rewarm remaining vegetable mixture in large nonstick skillet. Turn meatloaf out; cut into 1-inch-thick slices. Top with warm roasted vegetable mixture; serve with mashed potatoes.

6 SERVINGS

Using ground beef with a higher fat content ensures a moist meatloaf. Flaky panko crumbs are the best substitute for fresh breadcrumbs in almost anything, including meatloaf. Look for them in the Asian foods section of the supermarket and at Asian markets nationwide. Round out the meal with some boiled green beans.

Mustard Mashed Potatoes

2¾ pounds medium-size Yukon Gold potatoes, peeled, quartered
6 tablespoons (¾ stick) butter, room temperature
⅔ cup (or more) whole milk
3 tablespoons Dijon mustard

Cook potatoes in large pot of boiling salted water until very tender, about 25 minutes. Drain well. Return potatoes to pot. Add butter and mash potatoes until almost smooth. Mix in ⅔ cup milk and Dijon mustard. Season to taste with salt and pepper.

6 SERVINGS

Beer-Marinated Tri-Tip with Blue Cheese, Wild Mushrooms, and Onions

BEEF

- 1 12-ounce bottle of beer
- 1/3 cup pomegranate molasses*
- 4 large garlic cloves, chopped
- 2 teaspoons dried crushed red pepper
- 1 2 1/4-pound tri-tip beef roast, trimmed

MUSHROOMS AND ONIONS

- 2 large portobello mushrooms, stemmed, dark gills scraped out
- 8 ounces large fresh shiitake mushrooms, stemmed
- 6 ounces oyster mushrooms
- 1 12-ounce onion, peeled, cut into 1/2-inch-thick rounds
- 1/4 cup olive oil
- 6 garlic cloves, chopped
- 2 tablespoons balsamic vinegar

  Nonstick vegetable oil spray

- 2 cups low-salt chicken broth
- 1 cup beef broth
- 1/4 cup heavy whipping cream

- 1 cup crumbled blue cheese
- 1 tablespoon chopped fresh herbs

FOR BEEF: Combine first 5 ingredients in large heavy-duty resealable plastic bag; seal and shake to blend. Chill overnight.

FOR MUSHROOMS AND ONIONS: Place mushrooms and onions on rimmed baking sheet. Whisk oil, garlic, and vinegar in small bowl; season with salt and pepper. Brush vegetables with some dressing.

Spray grill rack with nonstick spray and prepare barbecue (medium-high heat). Grill mushrooms and onions until tender and lightly browned, turning occasionally, about 8 minutes. Return vegetables to same baking sheet; cut into 1/2-inch-thick strips.

Boil all broth in heavy large skillet over medium-high heat until reduced to 1 cup, about 12 minutes. Add cream, mushrooms, and onions. Boil until sauce coats vegetables, tossing occasionally, about 6 minutes. Season sauce to taste with salt and pepper. Set aside.

Drain marinade from beef into medium saucepan; boil 2 minutes. Cook beef over hottest part of grill until brown, about 5 minutes per side. Move beef to coolest part of grill; cover and cook until thermometer inserted into center registers 135°F for medium-rare, turning occasionally and basting with marinade, about 30 minutes. Transfer to cutting board; let rest 10 minutes.

Rewarm mushroom sauce. Thinly slice beef across grain. Overlap slices on platter. Spoon some sauce over; sprinkle with blue cheese and fresh herbs and serve.

A thick pomegranate syrup; sold at some supermarkets and Middle Eastern markets nationwide.

4 TO 6 SERVINGS

If you can find it, marinate the roast in a coffee porter (a dark beer that's flavored with coffee or with dark malts and highly roasted barley) or a similar beer with body, such as Guinness or a honey brown lager. Uncork an Australian Shiraz to go with the roast.

Mustard-Seed-Crusted Burgers with Horseradish Slaw

½ cup mayonnaise

½ cup sour cream

3 tablespoons prepared horseradish

1⅓ pounds ground beef

¼ cup yellow mustard seeds, coarsely crushed

1 tablespoon vegetable oil

4 kaiser rolls, halved horizontally

3 cups (about 6 ounces) thinly sliced iceberg lettuce

Serve these burgers with sliced onion and tomato if you like.

Whisk mayonnaise, sour cream, and horseradish in medium bowl to blend. Season with salt and pepper. Form ground beef into four ⅓-pound burgers, each about 3¾ inches in diameter and ½ inch thick. Sprinkle both sides of burgers with salt and pepper. Spread mustard seeds on small plate. Press both sides of burgers firmly into mustard seeds.

Heat vegetable oil in heavy large skillet over medium-high heat. Add burgers and cook until brown on both sides and pink in center, about 4 minutes per side. Arrange roll bottoms on each of 4 plates. Transfer burgers to roll bottoms. Stir lettuce into horseradish mixture to coat. Divide lettuce mixture atop hamburgers. Cover each burger with roll top and serve.

MAKES 4

Coconut Beef Curry on Chinese Egg Noodles

1 1⅓-pound flank steak, halved lengthwise, thinly cut crosswise on slight diagonal
1 tablespoon cornstarch
3 tablespoons vegetable oil
½ cup chopped shallots
1 tablespoon minced peeled fresh ginger
1 tablespoon Thai red curry paste*
1 teaspoon turmeric
1 13- to 14-ounce can unsweetened coconut milk
¼ cup fresh lime juice
4 teaspoons fish sauce (nam pla or nuoc nam)*
½ cup chopped fresh cilantro

¾ pound thin dried Chinese egg noodles
1 tablespoon Asian sesame oil

Place steak in large bowl; add cornstarch and toss to coat. Heat vegetable oil in large non-stick skillet over high heat. Add shallots, ginger, curry paste, and turmeric; stir 1 minute. Add steak; stir-fry until no longer pink, about 4 minutes. Add coconut milk, lime juice, and fish sauce. Simmer until sauce thickens, about 4 minutes. Mix in cilantro. Season curry with salt and pepper.

Meanwhile, cook noodles in large pot of boiling salted water until just tender, stirring often. Drain; toss with sesame oil. Serve curry atop noodles.

8 SERVINGS

Chipotle-Rubbed Steaks with Gorgonzola Toasts

4½ bay leaves
1½ tablespoons Hungarian sweet paprika
1½ teaspoons crushed chipotle chile pepper*
¾ teaspoon cumin seeds

4 1-inch-thick T-bone or rib steaks (about 1 pound each)

1 loaf ciabatta bread, halved horizontally, each half cut crosswise into eight 5x3-inch slices
   Olive oil
1 cup creamy Gorgonzola cheese
1 teaspoon chopped fresh thyme

Prepare barbecue (medium-high heat). Finely grind bay leaves, paprika, chipotle, and cumin seeds in spice grinder. Reserve 1 teaspoon mixture. Transfer remaining mixture to plate.

Sprinkle steaks generously with salt and pepper. Press both sides of steaks into spice mixture on plate and rub to spread evenly. Grill steaks to desired doneness, about 5 minutes per side for medium-rare.

Brush cut sides of bread with olive oil. Grill, cut side down, until slightly charred, about 1 minute. Spread Gorgonzola onto grilled side of each bread slice. Sprinkle cheese with ground black pepper and reserved spice mixture. Return bread to grill, cheese side up. Grill until cheese begins to melt and bottom of bread is slightly charred, about 1 minute. Sprinkle bread with thyme; place 2 slices on each of 4 plates. Serve steaks with bread.

Crushed chipotle chile pepper can be found in the spice section of most supermarkets.

4 SERVINGS

Grilled Hoisin-Soy Steaks with Shiitake and Bok Choy

4½ tablespoons mirin
1½ teaspoons Chinese five-spice powder, or 4 whole star anise, ground
3   tablespoons hoisin sauce
3   tablespoons toasted sesame seeds
3   tablespoons unseasoned rice vinegar
1½ tablespoons soy sauce
1½ tablespoons toasted sesame oil (such as Asian)
2   10- to 12-ounce rib-eye steaks
4   large shiitake mushrooms, stemmed
2   baby bok choy, quartered lengthwise

Prepare barbecue (medium-high heat). Mix first 7 ingredients in small saucepan; bring to boil. Cool. Place steaks, mushrooms, and bok choy on baking sheet. Pour half of sauce over; turn to coat. Reserve remaining sauce in same saucepan. Sprinkle steaks evenly with salt and pepper.

Grill steaks, mushrooms, and bok choy until meat is medium-rare and vegetables are partially charred, turning occasionally, about 10 minutes for steaks, 8 minutes for mushrooms, and 5 minutes for bok choy. Slice steaks; divide between 2 plates with mushrooms and bok choy. Bring remaining sauce to simmer; drizzle sauce over steak slices, mushrooms, and bok choy and serve.

2 SERVINGS

Veal Chops with Roasted Tomatoes, Arugula, and Soft Polenta

1   cup olive oil, divided
½   cup fresh lemon juice
¼   cup fresh thyme leaves
1   tablespoon coarse kosher salt
1   tablespoon ground black pepper
4   1¾-inch-thick veal rib chops (each about 12 ounces), frenched

18 small shallots, peeled, halved
¼   cup balsamic vinegar
1   12-ounce package grape tomatoes
⅓   cup drained capers plus 1 tablespoon caper brine reserved from jar

Soft Polenta (see recipe)
4   cups arugula

Whisk ¾ cup oil and lemon juice in small bowl to blend. Mix thyme, salt, and pepper in another small bowl. Rub thyme mixture all over veal chops; place in glass baking dish. Pour oil-lemon marinade over; let stand 15 minutes.

Preheat oven to 450°F. Combine shallots, vinegar, and remaining ¼ cup oil in medium roasting pan; toss to coat. Sprinkle with salt and pepper. Roast until shallots are browned and tender, about 15 minutes. Add tomatoes to shallots and roast until tomatoes are soft and browned, stirring occasionally, about 15 minutes longer. Remove pan from oven. Add capers and 1 tablespoon reserved brine; stir to blend.

Meanwhile, heat large ovenproof skillet over high heat. Drain veal chops and transfer marinade to heavy small saucepan. Add veal to skillet; cook until browned, 3 minutes per side. Transfer skillet to oven and roast veal to desired doneness, about 10 minutes for medium.

Bring reserved oil-lemon marinade to boil; boil 2 minutes. Place 1 veal chop on each of 4 plates. Divide shallot-tomato mixture among plates. Spoon Soft Polenta alongside. Drizzle with oil-lemon marinade. Garnish with arugula and serve.

4 SERVINGS

Ask your butcher to french (trim the fat from) the bone end of the veal rib chops.

Soft Polenta

  6 cups water
¼ cup (½ stick) butter
  1 teaspoon salt
1¼ cups quick-cooking polenta*

Bring 6 cups water, ¼ cup butter, and 1 teaspoon salt to boil in heavy large saucepan. Gradually whisk in polenta. Reduce heat to medium-low. Stir constantly until polenta thickens, about 5 minutes.

Quick-cooking polenta (precooked maize meal) is available at some supermarkets and at Italian markets.

4 SERVINGS

Veal Roasted with Shallots, Fennel, and Vin Santo

1	tablespoon coarse kosher salt
1	tablespoon dried thyme
½	teaspoon ground white pepper
4	tablespoons olive oil, divided
1	3¼-pound boneless veal shoulder roast
2	pounds shallots, thinly sliced
7½	cups thinly sliced fresh fennel (from 3 large bulbs)
1	500-ml bottle Vin Santo
1	tablespoon chopped fresh thyme

Look for fresh green shallots with glossy tight skins at farmers' markets. Vin Santo, Tuscany's celebrated dessert wine, lends its sweet, nutty flavor to the dish. Sautéed spinach would be a colorful side.

Preheat oven to 375°F. Mix salt, dried thyme, and white pepper in small bowl. Rub 1 tablespoon oil over roast. Rub salt mixture over roast. Heat 2 tablespoons olive oil in heavy large pot over medium-high heat. Add meat and cook until golden brown on all sides, about 5 minutes. Transfer roast to plate.

Add remaining 1 tablespoon oil, shallots, and fennel to same pot. Sauté until vegetables are golden brown, stirring frequently and scraping up browned bits, about 12 minutes. Add Vin Santo; boil 3 minutes. Return veal to pot, nestling into vegetables, and top with some of vegetables. Cover; roast until instant-read thermometer inserted into center of veal registers 165°F, about 1 hour 15 minutes.

Transfer veal to platter. Mix fresh thyme into vegetables. Season cooking liquid with salt and pepper. Spoon vegetables and cooking liquid around roast.

6 TO 8 SERVINGS

Wine-Braised Leg of Lamb with Garlic

1   5¾-pound bone-in leg of lamb, well trimmed
4   large garlic cloves, minced, divided
3   large heads of garlic, cut horizontally in half
1   bunch fresh thyme (about 1 ounce)
1   750-ml bottle dry white wine (such as Chardonnay)

2   tablespoons (¼ stick) butter

Preheat oven to 475°F. Place lamb in large roasting pan. Rub all over with half of minced garlic. Sprinkle with salt and pepper. Place halved heads of garlic around lamb, cut side up. Scatter thyme over and around lamb. Roast 20 minutes. Reduce oven temperature to 350°F.

Boil wine in large saucepan for 5 minutes. Pour around lamb. Cover; roast until lamb is very tender, about 2 hours 45 minutes longer. *(Can be made 1 day ahead. Cool, uncovered, 1 hour. Cover; chill. Rewarm, covered, in 350°F oven for 30 minutes before continuing.)*

Transfer lamb and heads of garlic to platter. Tent with foil. Using slotted spoon, remove thyme sprigs and garlic skins from pan juices. Place roasting pan over medium-high heat on stovetop. Bring juices to boil. Add butter and remaining minced garlic. Boil until juices thicken slightly, about 12 minutes. Season jus with salt and pepper. Slice lamb; arrange on platter. Spoon jus over and serve.

6 SERVINGS

Two elements make this dish special. Usually the smaller shanks are braised, but a whole leg works just as well and looks more impressive. Also, white wine is used for the braising instead of red. When ready to serve, however, uncork a full-bodied Zinfandel.

Lamb Chops with Feta and Banyuls-Cherry Sauce

¼	cup extra-virgin olive oil
2	garlic cloves, minced
1	tablespoon chopped fresh thyme
8	4-ounce lamb loin chops
1	cup dried tart cherries (about 6 ounces)
1	cup Banyuls vinegar* or Sherry wine vinegar
½	cup low-salt chicken broth
2	tablespoons brown sugar
3	tablespoons butter
⅔	cup crumbled feta cheese

Dried cherries are simmered in Banyuls vinegar and brown sugar, creating a sweet-sour sauce for the lamb.

Preheat oven to 400°F. Combine olive oil, minced garlic, and chopped thyme in small bowl. Rub all over lamb; season with salt and pepper. Transfer to baking sheet.

Meanwhile, combine cherries, vinegar, broth, and sugar in small saucepan. Bring to boil over medium-high heat, stirring until sugar dissolves. Reduce heat to medium-low; simmer until liquid is slightly reduced, about 15 minutes. Stir in butter. Season with salt and pepper.

Bake lamb 10 minutes. Top with cheese; bake until melted, about 5 minutes longer. Serve lamb with sauce.

An oak-aged vinegar available at specialty foods stores.

4 SERVINGS

Roast Leg of Lamb with Mint, Parsley, and Lima Bean Puree

¼ cup olive oil
¼ cup finely chopped fresh mint
¼ cup finely chopped fresh parsley
1 tablespoon minced fresh rosemary
2 garlic cloves, minced
1 5¼-pound boneless leg of lamb, butterflied, trimmed of most fat and sinew
Coarse kosher salt

Fresh mint sprigs
Lima Bean Puree (see recipe)

Preheat oven to 450°F. Mix oil, chopped mint, parsley, rosemary, and garlic in small bowl. Place lamb, cut side up, on work surface. Sprinkle lamb generously with coarse salt and pepper and rub into meat. Spread herb mixture over top of lamb, then roll up, enclosing herb mixture completely. Sprinkle outside of lamb with coarse salt and pepper. Tie lamb with kitchen string at 2-inch intervals. Place lamb in roasting pan. Roast until instant-read thermometer inserted into thickest part of meat registers 130°F for medium-rare, about 1 hour 15 minutes. Remove pan from oven; let lamb rest 15 minutes.

Remove kitchen string from lamb. Cut lamb into ¾-inch-thick slices; arrange on platter. Garnish with mint sprigs. Serve with Lima Bean Puree.

8 SERVINGS

Lima Bean Puree

6 cups water
3 10-ounce packages frozen baby lima beans
2 garlic cloves, minced
1 large fresh rosemary sprig
5 tablespoons butter, room temperature

Combine 6 cups water, lima beans, garlic, and rosemary sprig in large saucepan. Boil until beans are very soft, about 20 minutes. Drain, reserving cooking liquid. Discard rosemary sprig. Transfer bean mixture to processor. Add butter and puree until smooth, adding some of reserved cooking liquid by tablespoonfuls as needed to moisten. Season with salt and pepper. (*Can be prepared 2 hours ahead. Let stand at room temperature. Rewarm over medium heat, stirring occasionally and adding more reserved cooking liquid as needed to moisten.*)

8 SERVINGS

Lamb Chops with Meyer Lemon Compote

    ¾ cup dry white wine
    ½ cup sugar
    ¼ cup (packed) fresh mint leaves

    2 Meyer lemons*
    ¼ teaspoon coarse kosher salt

    8 ¾-inch-thick lamb rib or loin chops
    2 tablespoons vegetable oil

Combine wine, sugar, and mint in heavy small saucepan. Bring to boil, stirring until sugar dissolves. Remove from heat; let stand 30 minutes. Strain syrup into medium saucepan; discard mint.

Using vegetable peeler, remove peel from lemons in strips. Place strips in mini processor. Cut away all white pith from lemons and discard. Working on plate to catch juice, quarter lemons; remove seeds. Add lemons and juice to mini processor; using on/off turns, chop coarsely. Add lemon mixture to mint syrup. Boil until mixture is reduced to ⅔ cup, about 10 minutes. Stir in salt. Cool.

Sprinkle lamb with salt and pepper. Heat 1 tablespoon oil in each of 2 large skillets over medium-high heat. Add lamb; cook to desired doneness, about 2½ minutes per side for medium-rare. Serve lamb with compote.

Available at some supermarkets, farmers' markets, and specialty foods stores.

4 SERVINGS

Roast Pork Chops with Bacon and Wilted Greens

    2 1½-inch-thick rib pork chops
    3 tablespoons chopped fresh marjoram, divided
    ½ teaspoon ground allspice
    2 tablespoons olive oil

    2 thick-cut bacon slices, chopped
    2 garlic cloves, pressed
    8 cups (packed) wide strips assorted greens such as mustard greens and red Swiss chard,
         stems discarded
    5 teaspoons Sherry wine vinegar, divided
    ½ cup low-salt chicken broth
    2 tablespoons Dijon mustard

Preheat oven to 475°F. Sprinkle both sides of pork with 2 tablespoons marjoram, allspice, and generous amount of salt and pepper. Heat oil in heavy large nonstick skillet over high heat. Add pork and brown well, including edges, turning with tongs, about 7 minutes. Transfer pork to small rimmed baking sheet; reserve skillet. Roast pork in oven until thermometer inserted into center of chops from side registers 145°F, about 9 minutes.

Meanwhile, add bacon to oil in reserved skillet. Sauté over medium heat until brown, about 3 minutes. Mix in garlic. Add greens. Cook until just wilted, turning with tongs, about 3 minutes. Add 1 teaspoon vinegar; season with salt and pepper. Using tongs, transfer greens to colander to drain, leaving some bacon pieces in skillet for sauce. Add broth, mustard, and 4 teaspoons vinegar to skillet. Simmer until slightly thickened, about 4 minutes. Mix in 1 tablespoon marjoram. Season with salt and pepper.

Mound greens on plates; top with pork. Spoon sauce alongside.

2 SERVINGS

Grilled Ham and Gouda Sandwiches with Frisée and Caramelized Onions

1 tablespoon extra-virgin olive oil

1 large onion, thinly sliced

Unsalted butter, room temperature

4 ⅓-inch-thick slices country white bread or sourdough bread

4 ounces thinly sliced smoked ham, divided

3 ounces Gouda cheese, thinly sliced, divided

2 large handfuls frisée, torn into bite-size pieces (about 1 cup), divided

Heat oil in large nonstick skillet over medium heat. Add onion; sauté 5 minutes. Reduce heat to medium-low; cover and cook until onion is very tender and golden, stirring frequently, about 25 minutes longer. Season with salt and pepper. Cool slightly.

Butter 2 bread slices. Place bread, buttered side down, on platter. Divide onion, ham, cheese, and frisée between bread slices. Top each with another bread slice; butter top slices.

Heat another large nonstick skillet over medium heat. Add sandwiches and cook until bread is golden brown and cheese melts, pressing occasionally with spatula, about 4 minutes per side. Cut sandwiches in half diagonally and serve.

2 SERVINGS

Grilled Pork Chops with
Chunky Andouille Barbecue Sauce

Nonstick vegetable oil spray

1½ cups diced andouille sausage (about 7 ounces)

1½ cups chopped onion

2 cups tomato sauce

¼ cup balsamic vinegar

1 tablespoon dark brown sugar

2 teaspoons chili powder

1 teaspoon ground cumin

6 1-inch-thick rib pork chops
Additional chili powder and ground cumin

Spray grill rack with nonstick spray and prepare barbecue (medium heat). Sauté sausage and onion in heavy large saucepan over medium-high heat until onion begins to brown, about 8 minutes. Add tomato sauce, vinegar, sugar, 2 teaspoons chili powder, and 1 teaspoon cumin. Bring to boil; remove from heat.

Meanwhile, sprinkle chops on both sides with salt, then chili powder and cumin. Grill chops until cooked through but not dry, about 9 minutes per side. Serve with sauce.

6 SERVINGS

Brown Sugar and Bourbon Ribs

BASTING SAUCE

- ½ cup (packed) golden brown sugar
- ½ cup apple butter
- ¼ cup bourbon whiskey
- ¼ cup apple cider vinegar
- 3 tablespoons apple cider
- 2 tablespoons Dijon mustard

RIBS

- 1 tablespoon coarse kosher salt
- 1 tablespoon (packed) golden brown sugar
- 1½ teaspoons dry mustard
- 1½ teaspoons dried thyme
- 1 teaspoon ground ginger
- ½ teaspoon ground cinnamon
- ½ teaspoon cayenne pepper
- 2 2- to 2¼-pound racks baby back pork ribs

- 1 large onion, sliced
- 1 cinnamon stick, broken in half
- 6 thin rounds peeled fresh ginger
- 1¼ cups apple cider

Be sure to remove (or score) the membrane on the underside of the ribs so that the seasonings can penetrate and fully flavor the meat. Even better, ask the butcher to remove the membrane for you.

FOR BASTING SAUCE: Whisk all ingredients in medium bowl to blend.

FOR RIBS: Mix first 7 ingredients in small bowl. Using small sharp knife, loosen membrane from underside of each rib rack and pull off (or score membrane). Rub 1 tablespoon seasoning mix into each side of each rib rack. Place ribs in large roasting pan. Cover and chill at least 6 hours and up to 1 day.

Preheat oven to 325°F. Lift ribs from pan. Scatter onion, cinnamon stick, and ginger in pan. Pour in cider. Return ribs, meat side down, to pan; cover pan with foil. Roast ribs until meat is tender and begins to pull away from bones, about 2 hours. Uncover; cool at least 30 minutes and up to 2 hours.

Prepare barbecue (medium-high heat). Grill ribs until heated through and slightly charred, about 5 minutes per side. Brush generously on all sides with basting sauce. Grill until sauce becomes sticky glaze, about 3 minutes longer per side. Transfer rib racks to cutting board. Cut racks between bones into individual ribs. Arrange on platter and serve, passing remaining sauce separately.

4 SERVINGS

Roast Pork Tenderloin with Fresh and Dried Fruit

- 2   1-pound pork tenderloins
- 2½ teaspoons chopped fresh rosemary, divided
- 2   tablespoons olive oil
- 4   large shallots, chopped
- ¾ cup diced dried apples
- ¼ pound kumquats, quartered, seeded
- ½ cup fresh cranberries or frozen, thawed
- 1½ cups low-salt chicken broth
- ½ cup dry white wine

Preheat oven to 375°F. Sprinkle pork with 2 teaspoons rosemary, salt, and pepper. Heat olive oil in large ovenproof skillet over medium-high heat. Add pork (cut to fit, if necessary) and brown on all sides, about 10 minutes. Transfer pork to plate. Add chopped shallots to skillet and sauté 4 minutes. Add apples, kumquats, and cranberries; stir until heated through. Add chicken broth, wine, and ½ teaspoon rosemary. Boil 1 minute. Return pork and any juices to skillet, turning to coat with juices.

Place skillet in oven and roast pork until thermometer inserted into center registers 145°F to 150°F, about 25 minutes. Transfer pork to platter; let stand 10 minutes. If thicker sauce is desired, boil juices in skillet until reduced enough to coat spoon. Season sauce to taste with salt and pepper. Slice pork crosswise and spoon sauce over.

6 SERVINGS

Slow-Braised Pork with Black Grapes and Balsamic Vinegar

1 3¼-pound boneless pork shoulder (Boston butt), trimmed, cut into 3 equal pieces

4 tablespoons extra-virgin olive oil, divided

8 large shallots, halved, cut into ¼-inch-thick slices (about 3 cups)

3 cups seedless black grapes (about 1 pound)

2 tablespoons sugar

½ cup balsamic vinegar

2 cups low-salt chicken broth

2 large fresh sage sprigs

4 large fresh thyme sprigs

2 large fresh rosemary sprigs

The grapes and vinegar cook down into a sweet, complex sauce. The pork is perfect with a deep, concentrated red, like a California Zinfandel.

Preheat oven to 325°F. Sprinkle pork with salt and pepper. Heat 2 tablespoons oil in heavy large ovenproof pot over medium-high heat. Add pork to pot and cook until browned on all sides, about 13 minutes total. Transfer pork to plate; discard fat in pot.

Heat remaining 2 tablespoons oil in same pot over medium heat. Add shallots and grapes; sauté until shallots are golden, stirring occasionally, about 3 minutes. Add sugar; sauté 30 seconds. Add vinegar; bring mixture to boil and cook until slightly reduced, about 3 minutes. Add broth, all herb sprigs, and pork with juices from plate. Bring to boil. Cover pot and transfer to oven. Braise pork 1 hour. Using tongs, turn pork over and continue braising until meat is very tender, about 45 minutes longer. Using slotted spoon, transfer pork to platter; tent with aluminum foil.

Remove herb sprigs from pot and skim fat from surface of cooking liquid. Boil cooking liquid over high heat until thickened, about 7 minutes. Season sauce with salt and pepper. Pour over pork and serve.

4 TO 6 SERVINGS

Herb-Brined Pork Loin Rib Roast

BRINE

- 6 quarts cold water, divided
- 1½ cups sugar
- ¾ cup fine sea salt
- 8 large fresh thyme sprigs
- 6 Turkish bay leaves, crumbled
- 4 juniper berries*
- 2 teaspoons whole black peppercorns

PORK

- 1 6- to 6½-pound center-cut pork rib roast (8-bone; about 12 to 14 inches long), well-trimmed

- 2 tablespoons chopped fresh thyme
- 2 teaspoons whole black peppercorns, crushed in mortar with pestle or in resealable plastic bag with mallet

FOR BRINE: Combine 1 quart water and all remaining ingredients in medium saucepan. Bring to boil, stirring until sugar and salt dissolve. Pour brine into wide pot or container large enough to hold pork (3- to 4-gallon capacity). Add remaining 5 quarts cold water; stir to blend. Let stand until brine is cool to touch, about 1 hour.

FOR PORK: Place pork on work surface. Trim off all but ¼-inch layer of fat from roast. Turn roast over so that rib bones point up. Using boning knife and starting where meat meets rib bones, gradually cut loin away from rack of bones, leaving 2 inches of meat attached to bones (do not cut meat off bones completely). Tie meat back onto bones with kitchen string at 2-inch intervals. Place roast in brine, submerging pork completely and weighing down with heavy pot if necessary. Cover and refrigerate 5 days.

Remove pork from brine; discard brine. Rinse pork under cold running water for 5 minutes to reduce saltiness; pat dry with paper towels. Place pork on rack set over sheet of foil; let stand at room temperature 2 hours.

Position rack in center of oven and preheat to 400°F. Place pork on rack in large roasting pan. Mix thyme and crushed peppercorns in small bowl; sprinkle mixture over pork. Roast until instant-read thermometer inserted into center of pork registers 140°F, about 1 hour. Remove from oven. Let roast rest 30 minutes (internal temperature of roast will increase 5 to 10 degrees).

Remove kitchen string from roast. Cut meat into slices and serve.

Available in the spice section of most supermarkets.

8 SERVINGS

Pan-Seared Pork Tenderloin with Rhubarb Compote

6 tablespoons olive oil, divided

1½ tablespoons ground black pepper

1 tablespoon salt

2 teaspoons dried rubbed sage

2 teaspoons fennel seeds, ground in spice mill or in mortar with pestle

2½ pounds pork tenderloins (about 2 large or 3 medium), trimmed of fat and sinew

2 tablespoons chopped fresh parsley

Fresh sage sprigs

Rhubarb Compote (see recipe)

Orzo with lemon zest and Italian parsley would be lovely alongside. Uncork a Viognier or French Chardonnay.

Mix 3 tablespoons olive oil, ground black pepper, salt, dried sage, and ground fennel in small bowl. Rub oil mixture all over pork tenderloins; place in large baking dish and let stand 20 minutes.

Heat remaining 3 tablespoons oil in large nonstick skillet over medium-high heat. Add pork and cook until browned on all sides, about 6 minutes. Reduce heat to medium; cover and cook until instant-read thermometer inserted into center of pork registers 150°F, turning pork occasionally, about 8 minutes longer for medium tenderloins and 10 minutes for large.

Transfer pork to cutting board; let rest 5 minutes. Cut pork crosswise into ½-inch-thick slices; arrange on platter. Sprinkle with parsley; garnish with sage sprigs. Serve with Rhubarb Compote.

6 SERVINGS

Rhubarb Compote

6 cups 1-inch pieces fresh rhubarb (from about 2 pounds)

1¼ cups sugar

⅓ cup water

Combine all ingredients in heavy large saucepan. Bring to boil, stirring until sugar dissolves. Reduce heat to medium-low; simmer until rhubarb is very soft and begins to fall apart, stirring occasionally, about 20 minutes. Transfer compote to medium bowl. Refrigerate uncovered until cold, about 3 hours. (*Can be prepared 2 days ahead. Cover and keep chilled.*) Serve cold.

MAKES ABOUT 3 CUPS

Roasted Chicken with Moroccan Spices

3 tablespoons olive oil
3 tablespoons fresh lemon juice
2 tablespoons Hungarian sweet paprika
1 tablespoon ras-el-hanout*
1 tablespoon chopped fresh mint
1 tablespoon salt
2 teaspoons grated lemon peel
1 teaspoon ground black pepper
1 garlic clove, peeled

1 4¾- to 5-pound whole chicken
2 small whole lemons, pierced all over with fork
6 garlic cloves, unpeeled

Position rack in center of oven and preheat oven to 400°F. Blend first 9 ingredients in blender to form moist paste.

Remove neck, giblets, and excess fat from main cavity of chicken. Rinse chicken inside and out; pat dry with paper towels. Rub ⅓ of spice paste into main cavity and neck cavity, then rub remaining spice paste all over outside of chicken. Place lemons and garlic cloves in main cavity of chicken. Tie legs together. Place chicken on rack in roasting pan. Roast 45 minutes; tent with foil to prevent overbrowning. Continue to roast chicken until instant-read thermometer inserted into thickest part of thigh registers 170°F, about 45 minutes. Transfer chicken to platter; let stand 10 minutes (internal temperature will increase 5 to 10 degrees). Carve chicken and serve.

*A Moroccan spice blend available at some specialty foods stores and Middle Eastern markets.

4 SERVINGS

Chicken with Green Olives, Orange, and Sherry

2   tablespoons olive oil
1   4¾-pound chicken, cut into 8 pieces
1   cup sliced shallots (about 3 large)
2   garlic cloves, minced
1   cup medium Sherry
1   cup low-salt chicken broth
1   orange, halved lengthwise, each half cut into 5 wedges
⅓   cup brine-cured green olives (such as picholine)

1   tablespoon honey

Preheat oven to 425°F. Heat oil in large ovenproof skillet over high heat. Sprinkle chicken with salt and pepper. Add chicken to skillet; cook until skin is crisp and browned, about 6 minutes per side. Transfer chicken to plate. Reduce heat to medium-high. Drain all but 2 tablespoons drippings from skillet. Add shallots; stir until soft and beginning to brown, about 2 minutes. Add garlic; stir 30 seconds. Add Sherry; boil until reduced by half, scraping up browned bits, about 3 minutes. Add chicken broth; bring to boil. Return chicken, skin side up, to skillet. Place orange wedges and olives among chicken pieces. Transfer to oven; braise uncovered until chicken is cooked through, about 20 minutes.

Transfer chicken to platter. Bring sauce to boil over high heat. Stir in honey; boil until thickened, about 5 minutes. Season with salt and pepper. Pour sauce, oranges, and olives over chicken, or return chicken to skillet and serve.

4 SERVINGS

Chicken with Tangerine, Honey, and Chipotle Glaze

GLAZE

- 2 cups fresh tangerine juice
- 5 tablespoons honey
- ¼ cup soy sauce
- 2 tablespoons finely grated tangerine peel or orange peel
- 2 teaspoons minced canned chipotle chiles in adobo sauce*

CHICKEN

- 1 cup fresh tangerine juice or orange juice
- ⅓ cup chopped fresh parsley
- ⅓ cup chopped fresh cilantro
- 3 tablespoons chopped fresh thyme
- 3 tablespoons minced peeled fresh ginger
- 3 tablespoons unseasoned rice vinegar
- 2 tablespoons olive oil
- 2 tablespoons finely grated tangerine peel or orange peel
- 1 teaspoon coarse kosher salt
- 1 2¾- to 3-pound chicken, quartered, backbone removed

  Nonstick vegetable oil spray

FOR GLAZE: Boil juice, honey, and soy sauce in heavy medium saucepan until reduced to ⅔ cup, about 20 minutes. Mix in grated peel and chipotle chiles.

FOR CHICKEN: Whisk first 9 ingredients in 13x9x2-inch glass baking dish to blend. Add chicken; turn to coat. Cover; chill at least 2 hours and up to 1 day, turning occasionally.

Spray grill rack with nonstick spray and prepare barbecue (medium-low heat). Remove chicken from marinade; discard marinade. Sprinkle chicken lightly with salt. Grill chicken until cooked through, turning and repositioning occasionally for even cooking, about 20 minutes. Brush chicken all over with glaze; grill 2 minutes longer on each side. Transfer chicken to platter. Serve, passing remaining glaze separately.

Chipotle chiles are dried, smoked jalapeños canned in a spicy tomato sauce, which is sometimes called adobo. They are available at some supermarkets, specialty foods stores, and Latin markets.

4 SERVINGS

Parmesan-Crusted Chicken and Asparagus with Sauce Maltaise

  6 tablespoons (¾ stick) butter, divided

  3 large eggs
  3 tablespoons honey Dijon mustard
  2 cups panko* (Japanese breadcrumbs; about 3½ ounces)
1½ cups grated Parmesan cheese (about 4½ ounces)
1½ teaspoons salt
  1 teaspoon ground black pepper
  6 skinless boneless chicken breast halves, butterflied

  1 large bunch watercress, thick stems trimmed
     Asparagus with Sauce Maltaise (see recipe)

Preheat oven to 500°F. Butter large rimmed baking sheet with 2 tablespoons butter. Melt remaining 4 tablespoons butter in small saucepan; set melted butter aside.

Whisk eggs and mustard in bowl to blend. Mix panko, Parmesan, salt, and pepper in large bowl. Dip chicken into egg mixture, then panko mixture, coating generously. Place on prepared baking sheet. Drizzle reserved melted butter over chicken. Bake chicken until browned and cooked through, turning once, about 10 minutes.

Garnish chicken with trimmed watercress; serve chicken with Asparagus with Sauce Maltaise.

Sold in the Asian foods section of some supermarkets and at Asian markets.

6 SERVINGS

Asparagus with Sauce Maltaise

4   large egg yolks
¼   cup water
2   tablespoons fresh lemon juice
1½ cups (3 sticks) butter, melted, very hot
1   teaspoon grated orange peel

1¾ pounds medium asparagus spears, tough ends trimmed

Whisk egg yolks, ¼ cup water, and lemon juice in medium metal bowl to blend. Place bowl over large saucepan of barely simmering water. Whisk constantly until instant-read thermometer inserted into mixture registers 160°F, about 5 minutes. Transfer yolk mixture to blender. With blender running, gradually pour hot melted butter through opening in top of blender and blend until mixture is thick and creamy. Stir in orange peel. Season sauce with salt and pepper.

Meanwhile, cook asparagus in large saucepan of boiling salted water until crisp-tender, about 4 minutes. Drain; divide among plates. Spoon sauce over.

6 SERVINGS

Sauce Maltaise, a hollandaise flavored with orange juice and orange zest (though lemon juice adds a refreshing brightness in this version), is a classic accompaniment for asparagus. It also brings a note of luxury to chicken breasts baked with a panko-Parmesan crust. Ask your butcher to butterfly the chicken breasts. Serve the meal with an unoaked Chardonnay.

Chicken Cacciatore

1½	pounds plum tomatoes, coarsely chopped (scant 4 cups)
8	ounces crimini (baby bella) mushrooms
1	very large red onion, thinly sliced (about 3 cups)
5	tablespoons olive oil, divided
2	tablespoons Sherry wine vinegar
1	4½- to 4¾-pound chicken, cut into 8 pieces, excess fat trimmed
1½	tablespoons chopped fresh rosemary, divided
½	cup dry red wine
1	14½-ounce can diced tomatoes in juice
1	cup low-salt chicken broth
⅓	cup thinly sliced basil, divided
2	tablespoons drained capers, divided
12	ounces gemelli or penne, freshly cooked

Preheat oven to 400°F. Combine plum tomatoes, mushrooms, and onion in large bowl. Add 3 tablespoons oil and vinegar; toss to blend. Sprinkle generously with salt and pepper. Spread vegetable mixture in single layer on large rimmed baking sheet. Roast until onion slices are golden brown and all vegetables are tender, stirring frequently, about 50 minutes. Remove from oven and set aside. Reduce oven temperature to 350°F.

Sprinkle chicken with salt, pepper, and 1 tablespoon rosemary. Heat remaining 2 tablespoons oil in heavy large deep ovenproof skillet over medium-high heat. Add chicken and sauté until golden brown, about 6 minutes per side. Transfer chicken to bowl. Add wine to skillet and boil until wine is reduced by half, scraping up browned bits, about 1 minute. Stir in canned tomatoes with juice, then broth and bring to boil. Reduce heat to medium and simmer 10 minutes to blend flavors. Return chicken to sauce in skillet. Place skillet in oven and roast uncovered until chicken is cooked through and juices run clear when pierced with knife, about 25 minutes. Remove skillet from oven. Stir in roasted vegetables, remaining ½ tablespoon rosemary, half of basil, and half of capers. Simmer over medium heat until vegetables are heated through. Season with salt and pepper.

Place pasta in large shallow bowl. Top with chicken and sauce. Sprinkle remaining basil and capers over and serve.

6 SERVINGS

Chicken and Mushroom Pie with Phyllo-Parmesan Crust

1   ½-ounce package dried porcini
      mushrooms
1   cup hot water

9   tablespoons butter, divided
1   pound assorted fresh
      mushrooms (such as crimini,
      stemmed shiitake, and
      button mushrooms), sliced
3   garlic cloves, minced
2   cups low-salt chicken broth
¾   cup Riesling or other fruity
      white wine
2   ounces thin prosciutto slices,
      cut into thin strips
2   teaspoons grated lemon peel
2   teaspoons chopped fresh
      thyme
1   teaspoon salt
½   teaspoon ground black pepper
3   tablespoons cornstarch mixed
      with ½ cup water

12 sheets fresh phyllo pastry or frozen, thawed

2   pounds skinless boneless chicken thighs, excess fat removed, thighs quartered
2   tablespoons chopped fresh Italian parsley
½   cup finely grated Parmesan cheese

Combine dried porcini and 1 cup hot water in small bowl; let stand until porcini are soft, about 20 minutes. Drain porcini, reserving liquid.

Melt 3 tablespoons butter in heavy large pot over medium-high heat. Add fresh mushrooms and garlic; sauté until mushrooms are browned, about 8 minutes. Add porcini, porcini soaking liquid (leaving any sediment behind), broth, wine, prosciutto, lemon peel, thyme, 1 teaspoon salt, and ½ teaspoon pepper. Reduce heat to medium-low; simmer uncovered 20 minutes to blend flavors. Whisk cornstarch mixture to combine and add to skillet; stir until mixture thickens slightly, about 1½ minutes. Season sauce with more salt and pepper, if desired. (*Can be prepared 1 day ahead. Cool slightly, then cover and chill.*)

Preheat oven to 425°F. Melt 6 tablespoons butter in small saucepan; remove from heat. Place 1 phyllo sheet on work surface (cover remainder with sheet of plastic wrap, then damp towel). Brush phyllo sheet with some of melted butter. Using both hands, gently scrunch buttered phyllo sheet into loose ball, about 2½ to 3 inches in diameter; set on work surface. Repeat with remaining phyllo sheets and melted butter.

Bring mushroom sauce to boil. Mix in chicken and parsley. Transfer mixture to 13x9x2-inch glass or ceramic baking dish. Cover hot filling with phyllo balls. Sprinkle Parmesan over. Bake 15 minutes. Reduce oven temperature to 350°F; bake until phyllo is golden and chicken is cooked through, about 20 minutes longer.

6 SERVINGS

Boneless chicken thighs give a moist result, but chicken breasts work well, too. Mix wild mushrooms with cultivated button mushrooms for a deeper flavor.

Chicken Breasts with Pistachio-Cilantro Pesto

1   cup raw unsalted pistachios
2   cups (packed) fresh cilantro leaves
4   teaspoons fresh lemon juice, divided
1   garlic clove, chopped
1   teaspoon ground cardamom
¾   teaspoon salt
½   cup plus 5 tablespoons olive oil, divided

4   large chicken breast halves with skin and ribs attached

Preheat oven to 400°F. Toast pistachios on baking sheet until golden, about 7 minutes. Transfer to processor. Maintain oven temperature. Add cilantro leaves, 1 tablespoon lemon juice, garlic, cardamom, and ¾ teaspoon salt to processor. Using on/off turns, process until coarse paste forms. With machine running, gradually add ½ cup olive oil. Season with pepper.

Using fingers, gently loosen skin from 1 side of each chicken breast, forming pocket. Spread 1 tablespoon pesto evenly under skin of each. Sprinkle chicken generously with salt and pepper.

Heat 1 tablespoon olive oil in heavy large ovenproof skillet over medium-high heat. Add chicken, skin side down. Cook until skin is dark golden, about 5 minutes. Turn chicken over and transfer skillet to oven. Roast chicken until cooked through, about 25 minutes.

Place ½ cup remaining pesto into small bowl. Whisk in remaining ¼ cup olive oil and remaining 1 teaspoon lemon juice. Drizzle pesto sauce over chicken breasts and serve.

4 SERVINGS

Stir any remaining pesto into steamed vegetables or couscous.

Grilled Chicken with
Walnut-Pomegranate Sauce

SAUCE

- 3 tablespoons butter
- 2½ cups chopped onions
- 2 cups finely chopped walnuts
- ¼ cup pomegranate molasses*
- 2 tablespoons canned tomato sauce
- 2 tablespoons fresh lemon juice
- 1 tablespoon sugar
- ½ teaspoon ground cinnamon
- 2 cups (or more) low-salt chicken broth

CHICKEN

- ⅓ cup pomegranate molasses*
- ½ teaspoon ground cinnamon
- 6 large chicken breast halves with skin and bones

    Olive oil

    Mint sprigs

A grilled version of the classic Persian stew called *fesenjan*. Team it with carrot salad and a bottle of Cabernet Sauvignon.

FOR SAUCE: Melt butter in heavy large skillet over medium-high heat. Add onions; sauté 5 minutes. Add walnuts. Sauté until nuts are slightly darkened, about 12 minutes. Mix in pomegranate molasses, tomato sauce, lemon juice, sugar, and cinnamon, then 2 cups broth. Reduce heat to medium. Simmer until sauce thickens, about 15 minutes. Season with salt and pepper. *(Can be made 1 day ahead. Cover; chill. Rewarm, thinning with more broth, if desired.)*

FOR CHICKEN: Prepare barbecue (medium heat). Mix pomegranate molasses and cinnamon in small bowl for glaze. Brush chicken with oil; sprinkle with salt and pepper. Grill until just cooked through, turning often, about 35 minutes. Brush chicken all over with glaze; grill 2 minutes per side. Transfer to platter. Spoon some sauce over. Serve with remaining sauce. Garnish with mint.

A thick pomegranate syrup available at some supermarkets and at Middle Eastern markets.

6 SERVINGS

Cilantro-Lime Chicken Fajitas with Grilled Onions

  1¼ cups coarsely chopped fresh cilantro
  ¾ cup olive oil
  5 tablespoons fresh lime juice
  2½ teaspoons ground cumin
  1¼ teaspoons ancho chile powder

  6 skinless boneless chicken breast halves
  3 large fresh poblano chiles,* seeded, cut into ¾-inch-wide strips
  3 large yellow bell peppers, cut into ¾-inch-wide strips
  2 red onions, sliced into ½-inch rounds

  12 8-inch flour tortillas

     Optional toppings: purchased salsas, guacamole, sour cream, chopped fresh cilantro, sliced green onions, and chopped serrano chiles

Prepare barbecue (medium heat). Puree first 5 ingredients in processor. Season marinade with salt and pepper.

   Place chicken breast halves in 13x9x2-inch glass baking dish. Pour ⅓ cup marinade over; turn to coat. Arrange poblano chiles, bell peppers, and onions on large rimmed baking sheet. Pour ½ cup marinade over; turn to coat. Sprinkle chicken breasts and vegetables with salt and pepper. Reserve remaining marinade.

Grill chicken until cooked through, about 7 minutes per side. Grill vegetables until tender, turning frequently, about 15 minutes for onions and 12 minutes for poblanos and bell peppers. Grill tortillas until charred, about 1 minute per side.

Transfer chicken to work surface; slice crosswise into strips. Fill tortillas with chicken and vegetables; drizzle with reserved marinade. Serve with toppings.

Fresh, green chiles, often called pasillas; *available at some supermarkets and at Latin markets.*

6 SERVINGS

Chicken and White Bean Chili

¼ cup olive oil
1⅓ cups chopped onion
1 large green bell pepper, chopped
6 garlic cloves, chopped
2¼ pounds skinless boneless chicken thighs, cut into ½-inch cubes
3½ tablespoons chili powder
2 tablespoons tomato paste
1 tablespoon ground cumin
1 tablespoon dried oregano
2 15- to 16-ounce cans white beans, drained, juices reserved
2 15-ounce cans diced tomatoes in juice
½ cup chopped fresh cilantro

Heat oil in large pot over medium-high heat. Add onion, bell pepper, and garlic; sauté 5 minutes. Add chicken; sprinkle with salt and pep-

per and sauté 5 minutes longer. Mix in next 6 ingredients, including 1 cup reserved bean juices. Simmer until chicken is cooked through, about 25 minutes. If chili is too thick, add more bean juices by tablespoonfuls. Season to taste with salt and pepper. Mix in cilantro.

6 SERVINGS

Chips, Salsa, and Guacamole

Margaritas

Cilantro-Lime Chicken Fajitas with Grilled Onions
(opposite; pictured opposite)

Mixed Greens with Oranges, Watercress, and Onion
(page 147)

Spanish Rice

Mexican Beer

Lime Sorbet

Duck Stuffed with Chicken Liver, Candied Orange, and Pears

3 cups sugar

2²/₃ cups water

2 oranges, ends trimmed and discarded, each cut into 5 rounds

6 tablespoons extra-virgin olive oil, divided

14 ounces chicken livers, fat trimmed

10 large fresh sage leaves

2 garlic cloves, thinly sliced

2 cups diced peeled pears (about 2 medium)

2 cups dry red wine

2 4¹/₂- to 5-pound ducks, thawed if frozen, excess fat trimmed, rinsed, patted dry

2 tablespoons honey

Combine sugar and 2²/₃ cups water in heavy medium saucepan. Bring to simmer, stirring until sugar dissolves. Add orange slices and boil gently until orange peels are almost translucent, about 30 minutes. Drain. Place orange slices on rack set over plate and let drain another 30 minutes. Cut slices into ¹/₂-inch dice. (*Can be made 1 day ahead. Cover; chill.*)

Heat 4 tablespoons oil in large nonstick skillet over medium-high heat. Add chicken livers, sage, and garlic; sauté until livers are browned but still slightly pink inside, about 9 minutes. Remove from heat; cool slightly. Cut chicken livers into ¹/₂-inch dice; return to skillet. Mix in pears and diced candied oranges. Season stuffing with salt and pepper.

Preheat oven to 400°F. Boil wine in small saucepan for 3 minutes to allow alcohol to cook away; set aside. Sprinkle duck cavities with salt and pepper. Fill cavities with liver stuffing, dividing equally. Close cavity openings with small metal skewers. Place ducks in large roasting pan. Brush ducks with remaining 2 tablespoons oil. Sprinkle with salt and pepper. Roast ducks 20 minutes. Pour wine into roasting pan. Brush ducks with honey. Continue to roast until ducks are cooked through and juices run clear when thickest part of thigh is pierced with fork, about 1 hour 10 minutes longer. Transfer ducks to platter. Spoon fat off top of pan juices and discard. Pour pan juices into small bowl; season with salt and pepper. Serve ducks and stuffing with pan juices.

6 SERVINGS

The Ultimate Turkey

GRAVY BASE

   2 tablespoons (¼ stick) unsalted butter

   2 pounds turkey necks and/or wings

   2 cups diced onions

   1 cup diced peeled carrots

   1 cup diced celery

   6 cups (or more) low-salt chicken broth

TURKEY

   1 cup (2 sticks) butter, room temperature, divided

   2 teaspoons minced fresh thyme plus 15 fresh thyme sprigs

   2 teaspoons minced fresh tarragon plus 5 large fresh tarragon sprigs

   2 teaspoons minced fresh rosemary plus 5 fresh rosemary sprigs

   2 teaspoons minced fresh sage plus 5 fresh sage sprigs

   1 14- to 16-pound turkey

   4 cups low-salt chicken broth, divided

  ¼ cup all purpose flour

FOR GRAVY BASE: Melt butter in heavy large deep skillet over high heat. Add turkey necks and/or wings and sauté until deep brown, about 15 minutes. Add onions, carrots, and celery and sauté until vegetables are deep brown, about 15 minutes. Add 6 cups chicken broth and bring to boil. Reduce heat to medium-low and simmer uncovered 45 minutes, stirring occasionally.

Pour gravy base through strainer set over 4-cup measuring cup, pressing on solids to extract liquid. If necessary, add enough chicken broth to gravy base to measure 4 cups. *(Gravy base can be prepared 2 days ahead. Cool slightly. Refrigerate uncovered until cold, then cover and keep chilled. Rewarm before using.)*

FOR TURKEY: Mix ½ cup butter and all minced herbs in small bowl; season herb butter with salt and pepper. Transfer 2 generous tablespoons to another small bowl and reserve for gravy; let stand at room temperature.

Set rack at lowest position in oven and preheat to 425°F. Rinse turkey inside and out; pat dry. Starting at neck end, slide hand between skin and breast meat to loosen skin. Rub 4 tablespoons herb butter over breast meat under skin. Place turkey on rack set in large roasting pan. Sprinkle main cavity generously with salt and pepper. Place 4 tablespoons plain butter and all fresh herb sprigs in main cavity. Tuck wing tips under. Tie legs together loosely. Rub remaining herb butter over outside of turkey. Sprinkle turkey generously with salt and pepper.

Place turkey in oven and roast 20 minutes. Reduce oven temperature to 350°F. Roast turkey 30 minutes; pour 1 cup broth over and add 1 tablespoon plain butter to roasting

pan. Roast turkey 30 minutes; baste with pan juices, then pour 1 cup broth over and add 1 tablespoon butter to pan. Cover turkey loosely with foil. Roast turkey until thermometer inserted into thickest part of thigh registers 175°F, basting with pan juices and adding 1 cup broth and 1 tablespoon butter to pan every 45 minutes, about 1 hour 45 minutes longer. Transfer turkey to platter; let stand 30 minutes (internal temperature will rise 5 to 10 degrees).

Strain pan juices into bowl; whisk in gravy base. Melt reserved 2 tablespoons herb butter in heavy large saucepan over medium heat; add flour and whisk constantly until roux is golden brown, about 6 minutes. Gradually add pan juice-gravy base mixture; increase heat and whisk constantly until gravy thickens, boils, and is smooth. Reduce heat to medium; boil gently until gravy is reduced to 4½ cups, whisking often, about 10 minutes. Season gravy with salt and pepper.

8 SERVINGS

Thai-Curried Game Hens

3 tablespoons grapeseed oil or olive oil, divided
2 teaspoons (about) Thai red curry paste*
1 tablespoon tomato paste
1 cup canned unsweetened coconut milk*
1 cup low-salt chicken broth
2 5.95-ounce cans straw mushrooms, drained
3 kaffir lime leaves or 2 teaspoons grated lime peel
2 tablespoons fish sauce (such as nam pla or nuoc nam)*
1 tablespoon (packed) golden brown sugar
6 cherry tomatoes, quartered

2 1¼-pound Cornish game hens, thawed if frozen, halved lengthwise, backbones removed
Fresh basil leaves
Small fresh or dried red chiles** (optional garnish)

Heat 1 tablespoon oil in heavy medium saucepan over medium heat. Add curry paste and tomato paste and stir until fragrant, about 3 minutes. Add coconut milk, broth, mushrooms, kaffir lime leaves, fish sauce, and brown sugar; bring to simmer. Remove from heat. Add cherry tomatoes. Season sauce to taste with salt and pepper.

Preheat oven to 350°F. Heat 2 tablespoons oil in large nonstick skillet over high heat. Sprinkle hens with salt and pepper. Add hens to skillet and cook until browned, about 4 minutes per side. Transfer hens to 13x9x2-inch glass or ceramic baking dish. Pour sauce over. Bake uncovered until hens are cooked through, about 35 minutes. Transfer hens to shallow serving bowl; tent with foil. Skim fat from sauce. Pour sauce into large skillet; boil 5 minutes. Pour sauce over hens. Garnish with basil and chiles, if desired.

*Sold in the Asian foods section of many supermarkets and at Asian markets.
**Use any type of small fresh or dried chiles you find in the produce section or spice section of the supermarket.

4 SERVINGS

Curry pastes vary in strength and spiciness from brand to brand, so start by using one teaspoon if you prefer a milder sauce. Thanks to the purchased curry paste (now sold in many supermarkets), the delicious sauce has the complex, aromatic flavors of a Thai curry, but is very easy to prepare. Look for fresh or frozen kaffir lime leaves—their beautiful fragrance is the signature of many Thai dishes—at Asian markets. If unavailable, don't use dried ones; substitute grated lime peel instead.

Fennel- and Dill-Rubbed Grilled Salmon

1 tablespoon fennel seeds

¼ cup plus 2 teaspoons (packed) golden brown sugar

3 tablespoons Pimentón de la Vera (Spanish smoked paprika)*

1 tablespoon coarse kosher salt

2 teaspoons freshly ground black pepper

2 teaspoons dried dill weed

Nonstick vegetable oil spray

1 3¾- to 4-pound side of salmon with skin (preferably wild salmon)

Olive oil

Finely grind fennel seeds in spice mill or coffee grinder. Transfer to small bowl. Mix in next 5 ingredients.

Spray grill rack with nonstick spray. Prepare barbecue (medium-high heat). Brush salmon lightly on both sides with oil. Rub spice mixture generously over flesh side of salmon. Place salmon, skin side up, on grill rack; cover and cook until fish is slightly firmer, about 8 minutes. Slide rimless baking sheet under salmon to turn salmon over without breaking.

Place another rimless baking sheet atop salmon. Using both hands, firmly hold baking sheets together and invert salmon; slide salmon, flesh side up, off baking sheet and onto grill rack. Cover and grill until just opaque in center, about 8 minutes longer. Using rimless baking sheet, remove salmon from grill. Gently slide salmon, flesh side up, onto platter and serve.

Available at specialty foods stores.

8 SERVINGS

Be sure to buy the salmon with the skin on, which makes it much easier to handle as it grills. Keep in mind this is a special cut that your fish market or supermarket seafood counter may have to order. Serve this with grilled vegetables, coleslaw, and Chardonnay.

Grilled Fish Tostadas with Pineapple-Jicama Salsa

1½ cups diced peeled pineapple
1 cup diced peeled jicama
½ cup diced red onion
¼ cup chopped fresh cilantro
¼ cup fresh lime juice
2 serrano chiles, seeded, chopped

¼ cup olive oil
2 teaspoons chili powder
3 small zucchini (about 10 ounces), each cut lengthwise into 5 slices
1 pound halibut fillets
4 5- to 6-inch corn tortillas

Prepare barbecue (medium-high heat). Mix first 6 ingredients in medium bowl. Season salsa with salt and pepper.

Whisk oil and chili powder in small bowl. Arrange zucchini, fish, and tortillas in single layer on large baking sheet. Brush chili oil on both sides of zucchini, fish, and tortillas. Sprinkle zucchini and fish with salt and pepper. Grill until fish is cooked through and zucchini is tender, about 3 minutes per side. Grill tortillas until crisp, about 2 minutes per side. Divide zucchini among tortillas. Cut fish into strips and place atop zucchini. Top with salsa.

4 SERVINGS

Cedar-Planked Monkfish with Fire-Roasted Puttanesca Relish

1   untreated (about 12x10x1-inch) red cedar plank

3   tablespoons olive oil, divided
2   plum tomatoes, halved lengthwise
1   small sweet onion (such as Vidalia or Maui), quartered
1   large red bell pepper, halved lengthwise

½   cup Kalamata olives, pitted, coarsely chopped
3   anchovy fillets, finely chopped
2   garlic cloves, chopped
2   tablespoons chopped fresh basil
1   tablespoon drained capers
1   tablespoon white balsamic vinegar or unseasoned rice vinegar

4   6-ounce monkfish fillets
8   long thin slices prosciutto

Planking is an especially good technique for barbecuing fish, which has a tendency to flake and fall apart on the grill. Use a 1-inch-thick cedar plank for this recipe. Thinner planks have a tendency to burn and warp on the grill. You can buy them at barbecue stores or look for cedar marked "untreated" at lumberyards and some home-improvement stores. Begin soaking the cedar plank one day ahead. A German Riesling is ideal with this dish.

Fill roasting pan with water. Add cedar plank; weigh down with can or small pot to keep submerged and soak 1 day.

Prepare barbecue (high heat). Brush grill rack with 1 tablespoon oil. Arrange tomatoes, onion, and bell pepper on rimmed baking sheet. Sprinkle with salt and pepper; drizzle with 1 tablespoon oil. Grill vegetables until lightly charred and blistered, turning occasionally with tongs, about 4 minutes for tomatoes and 8 minutes for onion and pepper. Return vegetables to same sheet and cool slightly.

Peel tomato halves; peel pepper halves. Chop all vegetables coarsely and place in medium bowl. Add olives, anchovies, garlic, basil, capers, vinegar, and remaining 1 tablespoon oil. Toss to blend. Season relish to taste with salt and pepper. (Can be made 1 hour ahead. Let stand at room temperature.)

Sprinkle fillets with salt and pepper. Wrap 2 prosciutto slices around each fillet, leaving top and bottom exposed. Secure prosciutto with toothpicks. Press each fillet slightly to flatten top.

Drain cedar plank. Place fillets on plank. Spoon ¼ cup relish atop each fillet and press to adhere. Place plank on grill; cover barbecue. Cook fish until just opaque in center and thermometer inserted into center registers 120°F, checking occasionally and spraying plank with water if beginning to burn, about 18 minutes. Transfer fish to plates. Serve, passing remaining relish alongside.

4 SERVINGS

Salmon with Peas, Pea Tendrils, and Dill-Cucumber Sauce

2 tablespoons olive oil, divided
1 2½-pound center-cut wild salmon fillet, skin and pinbones removed
½ cup fresh orange juice
¼ cup fresh lemon juice
1 teaspoon coarse kosher salt

Peas and Pea Tendrils with Lemon Dressing (see recipe)
Dill-Cucumber Sauce (see recipe)

Brush small rimmed baking sheet with 1 tablespoon oil. Place salmon on prepared baking sheet. Mix orange juice and lemon juice in small bowl; pour over salmon. Drizzle 1 tablespoon oil over salmon; sprinkle with coarse salt and pepper. Let stand 15 minutes.

Preheat broiler. Broil salmon, without turning fish over, until just opaque in center, watching closely and turning baking sheet once for even broiling, about 12 minutes. Using 2 wide spatulas, transfer salmon to platter. Surround with Peas and Pea Tendrils with Lemon Dressing. Serve with Dill-Cucumber Sauce.

6 SERVINGS

Peas and Pea Tendrils with Lemon Dressing

¼ cup olive oil
2 tablespoons fresh lemon juice
1 teaspoon sugar

2 cups shelled fresh peas or one 10-ounce package frozen petite peas, unthawed
8 ounces pea tendrils, cut into 4-inch lengths

Whisk oil, lemon juice, and sugar in small bowl to blend; set dressing aside.

Bring large pot of salted water to boil. Add fresh or frozen peas and cook 3 minutes. Add pea tendrils; cook 1 minute. Drain well. Return vegetables to pot; add oil-lemon dressing and toss to coat. Season with salt and pepper.

6 SERVINGS

Dill-Cucumber Sauce

   1⅓ cups (packed) coarsely chopped fresh dill
    1 cup ½-inch cubes unpeeled English hothouse cucumber
   1½ tablespoons minced shallot
   ¼ teaspoon cayenne pepper
   ¾ cup mayonnaise
   ¾ cup sour cream

Blend dill, cucumber, shallot, and cayenne in processor until cucumber is finely chopped; transfer to medium bowl. Whisk in mayonnaise and sour cream. Season to taste with salt and pepper.

MAKES ABOUT 2 CUPS

Salmon with dill and cucumbers is updated with a very modern side dish—pea tendrils (the young leaves and shoots of snow pea plants) and peas, cooked quickly and tossed with a fresh lemon dressing. The salmon is equally good served hot or cold. Uncork Chardonnay or white Burgundy, such as Saint-Véran.

Ahi Tuna with Lemon Aioli and Couscous

  2 teaspoons fennel seeds
  1 teaspoon coriander seeds
  1 teaspoon whole black peppercorns
1½ teaspoons kosher salt, divided

  ⅓ cup mayonnaise
  2 tablespoons fresh lemon juice
  3 tablespoons chopped fresh chives
  4 garlic cloves, minced, divided

  ½ cup extra-virgin olive oil, divided
  1 carrot, peeled, coarsely chopped
  ¼ cup chopped red onion
  2 teaspoons chopped fresh thyme
2¼ cups water
  ½ pound sugar snap peas
  2 cups couscous
  2 tablespoons chopped fresh dill

2½ pounds ahi tuna steaks (about 1¼ inches thick)

Combine first 3 ingredients in heavy small skillet. Toast over medium heat until fragrant, shaking skillet occasionally, about 3 minutes. Grind spice mixture in spice grinder. Transfer to bowl; mix in 1 teaspoon salt.

Whisk mayonnaise, lemon juice, chives, and half of garlic in small bowl. *(Can be made 2 days ahead. Store spice mixture airtight at room temperature. Cover and refrigerate aioli.)*

Heat 2 tablespoons oil in heavy large skillet over medium-high heat. Add carrot and onion and sauté until crisp-tender, about 3 minutes. Add thyme and remaining garlic and sauté 1 minute. Add 2¼ cups water and remaining ½ teaspoon salt; bring to boil. Add sugar snap peas and cook until crisp-tender, about 1 minute. Using slotted spoon, transfer peas to plate. Immediately add couscous to water in skillet and stir to combine. Cover and remove from heat. Let stand 5 minutes. Fluff couscous with fork. Transfer to bowl and cool completely. Mix in sugar snap peas and dill. Season to taste with pepper. (*Couscous can be made 2 hours ahead. Let stand at room temperature.*)

Prepare barbecue (high heat). Coat tuna with 6 tablespoons oil. Sprinkle with spice mixture. Grill tuna until seared outside and rare in center, about 4 minutes per side. Refrigerate uncovered for 1 hour, then cut into ½-inch-thick slices. Spoon couscous onto plates. Top with tuna and drizzle with lemon aioli.

6 SERVINGS

Mahi-Mahi with Blood Orange, Avocado, and Red Onion Salsa

 1 blood orange, Cara Cara orange, or regular orange
 ½ cup ⅓-inch cubes avocado
 ⅓ cup chopped red onion
 2 teaspoons minced red jalapeño
 2 teaspoons fresh lime juice

 2 teaspoons olive oil
 2 6-ounce mahi-mahi fillets

Using small sharp knife, cut peel and white pith from orange. Working over small bowl, cut between membranes to release segments. Add avocado, onion, jalapeño, and lime juice to oranges in bowl; stir gently to blend. Season salsa to taste with salt.

Heat oil in heavy medium skillet over medium-high heat. Sprinkle fish with salt and pepper. Add fish to skillet and sauté until brown and cooked through, about 5 minutes per side.

Place 1 fillet on each of 2 plates. Spoon salsa atop fish and serve.

2 SERVINGS

Plank-Roasted Wild Salmon
with White Nectarine-Serrano Salsa

2 firm but ripe white nectarines (about 12 ounces), halved, pitted, cut into ¼-inch pieces
1 serrano chile, seeded, minced
1 tablespoon minced fresh cilantro
2 teaspoons minced fresh mint
2 teaspoons fresh lime juice
1 teaspoon sugar

1 cedar plank (approximately 10x17 inches)
4 6-ounce wild salmon fillets with skin

Combine first 6 ingredients in small bowl. Season salsa with salt and pepper. Cover with plastic wrap and chill. *(Can be made 3 hours ahead. Keep chilled.)*

Place cedar plank in oven; set oven at 250°F and let plank heat for 30 minutes. Sprinkle salmon with salt and pepper; place skin side down on heated cedar plank. Bake until salmon is just opaque in center, about 25 minutes. Transfer salmon to plates. Top with salsa.

4 SERVINGS

Grilled Halibut with Tatsoi and Spicy Thai Chiles

5 tablespoons sugar
5 tablespoons fish sauce (such as nam pla or nuoc nam)*
¼ cup water
3 tablespoons fresh lime juice
2 tablespoons minced peeled fresh ginger
2 garlic cloves, minced
2 Thai bird chiles with seeds or ½ large jalapeño chile with seeds, minced

1 small carrot, peeled, cut into matchstick-size strips
4 6- to 7-ounce halibut fillets
3 tablespoons vegetable oil, divided

1 shallot, thinly sliced
¾ pound tatsoi or baby spinach (about 12 cups packed)

Mix first 7 ingredients in medium glass bowl. Season with salt and pepper. *(Sauce can be prepared 2 days ahead. Cover and refrigerate.)*

Prepare barbecue (medium-high heat). Place carrot in medium bowl. Cover with ice water. Let stand 15 minutes, then drain well. Brush fish on all sides with 2 tablespoons oil. Sprinkle with salt and pepper. Grill until just opaque in center, about 4 minutes per side.

Meanwhile, heat 1 tablespoon oil in large nonstick skillet over medium heat. Add shallot; stir 1 minute. Add tatsoi; sprinkle with salt. Toss until tatsoi is wilted but still bright green, about 2 minutes; divide among 4 plates.

Place fish atop tatsoi. Sprinkle each fillet with carrot; drizzle each with 2 tablespoons sauce. Serve, passing remaining sauce separately.

Available in the Asian section of many supermarkets, at some specialty foods stores, and at Asian markets.

4 SERVINGS

The ginger sauce is a good staple to keep on hand in the fridge—it's excellent with any fish, whether grilled, pan-seared, or steamed. Serve rice on the side, if you like. *Tatsoi*, a relative of bok choy, grows very close to the ground with an open head similar to a blooming flower (hence its other name, rosette bok choy). With emerald-green leaves and pale-green stems, *tatsoi* has pronounced cabbage and mustard flavors.

Pan-Roasted Swordfish Steaks with Mixed-Peppercorn Butter

¼ cup (½ stick) butter, room temperature
2 teaspoons chopped fresh parsley
1 garlic clove, minced
½ teaspoon ground mixed peppercorns, plus more for sprinkling
½ teaspoon (packed) grated lemon peel

1 tablespoon olive oil
4 1-inch-thick swordfish fillets (about 6 ounces each)

Preheat oven to 400°F. Mash butter, parsley, garlic, ½ teaspoon ground mixed peppercorns, and lemon peel in small bowl. Season to taste with salt.

Heat oil in heavy large ovenproof skillet over medium-high heat. Sprinkle swordfish with salt and ground mixed peppercorns. Add swordfish to skillet. Cook until browned, about 3 minutes. Turn swordfish over and transfer to oven. Roast until just cooked through, about 10 minutes longer. Transfer swordfish to plates. Add seasoned butter to same skillet. Cook over medium-high heat, scraping up browned bits, until melted and bubbling. Pour butter sauce over swordfish and serve.

4 SERVINGS

Steamed Snapper with Ginger, Lime, and Cilantro

5 tablespoons chopped fresh cilantro, divided
¼ cup bottled clam juice
2 tablespoons fresh lime juice
2 tablespoons chopped green onion
1 tablespoon grated peeled fresh ginger
1 tablespoon soy sauce
1 tablespoon toasted sesame oil
1 teaspoon fish sauce (such as nam pla or nuoc nam)*

2 6- to 8-ounce red snapper fillets or halibut fillets

Mix 3 tablespoons cilantro and next 7 ingredients in small bowl to blend. Set aside. Pour enough water into large pot to reach depth of 1 inch. Add steamer rack or basket. Top with 9-inch-diameter glass pie dish. Bring water to boil.

Place fish in pie dish. Pour cilantro sauce over. Sprinkle with salt and pepper. Cover pot; steam fish just until opaque in center, about 6 minutes for snapper and 8 minutes for halibut. Serve with sauce; garnish with 2 tablespoons cilantro.

Available in the Asian foods section of many supermarkets, at some specialty foods stores, and at Asian markets.

2 SERVINGS

Seared Tuna on Fettuccine with Green Olives and Arugula

12 ounces fettuccine
1 cup green olive bruschetta spread from jar (about 8 ounces)
6 tablespoons olive oil, divided
4 teaspoons grated lemon peel, divided
4 teaspoons fresh lemon juice
1 5-ounce package baby arugula

2 12-ounce tuna steaks, each about 1 inch thick
4 teaspoons chopped fresh marjoram

Cook pasta in large pot of boiling salted water until tender but still firm to bite, stirring occasionally. Drain, reserving ½ cup pasta cooking liquid. Return pasta to pot. Add olive bruschetta spread, 3 tablespoons oil, 2 teaspoons lemon peel, lemon juice, and enough cooking liquid to coat. Season with salt and generous amount of pepper. Mix in arugula, which will wilt slightly.

Meanwhile, brush each tuna steak with 1 tablespoon oil; sprinkle with salt and pepper. Sprinkle both sides of tuna steaks evenly with marjoram and 2 teaspoons lemon peel; press gently to adhere.

Heat remaining 1 tablespoon oil in large nonstick skillet over high heat. Add tuna; sear until crusty and brown outside but still pink inside, about 1½ minutes per side. Transfer tuna to work surface; slice thinly. Divide pasta among plates; top with tuna slices.

4 SERVINGS

Dinner with the Neighbors for 4

Artichoke-Olive "Chips and Dip"
(page 17)

Martinis

Pan-Roasted Swordfish Steaks with Mixed-Peppercorn Butter
(opposite; pictured opposite)

Roasted Carrots, Parsnips, and Meyer Lemon
(page 138)

Steamed Rice

Chardonnay

Raspberries with Saba Sabayon
(page 211)

Baked Halibut with Orzo, Spinach, and Cherry Tomatoes

4 tablespoons extra-virgin olive oil, divided
2 tablespoons fresh lemon juice
2 6- to 7-ounce halibut fillets

1 cup orzo (rice-shaped pasta)
1 garlic clove, minced
4 cups (packed) baby spinach
1 cup halved cherry tomatoes

Preheat oven to 425°F. Whisk 2 tablespoons oil and lemon juice in bowl; season dressing with salt and pepper. Place halibut on rimmed baking sheet; sprinkle with salt and pepper. Drizzle with some of dressing. Bake until just opaque in center, about 12 minutes.

Meanwhile, cook pasta in large saucepan of boiling salted water until tender but still firm to bite; drain. Add 2 tablespoons oil and garlic to same saucepan; sauté over medium heat 1 minute. Add drained pasta, spinach, and tomatoes; stir to coat. Season with salt and pepper. Remove from heat. Cover; let stand 1 minute (spinach will wilt). Divide pasta between 2 plates. Top with halibut and remaining dressing.

2 SERVINGS

Chili-Garlic Shrimp with Mixed Greens, Avocado, and Corn

1 teaspoon chili-garlic sauce
½ teaspoon ground cumin
½ teaspoon kosher salt
¼ teaspoon plus ⅛ teaspoon ground black pepper
2 pounds uncooked large shrimp, peeled, deveined
5 tablespoons extra-virgin olive oil, divided

2 ears of corn, husked
3 small tomatoes, cut into ½-inch-thick wedges
⅓ English hothouse cucumber, halved lengthwise, thinly sliced crosswise

4 teaspoons fresh lime juice
2 teaspoons reduced-sodium soy sauce
1 teaspoon toasted sesame oil (such as Asian)

1 large avocado, halved, peeled, pitted, cut into thin slices
8 cups (loosely packed) mixed baby greens
2 tablespoons thinly sliced fresh mint leaves

Mix chili-garlic sauce, cumin, ½ teaspoon salt, and ¼ teaspoon pepper in large bowl. Add shrimp and toss to coat. Heat 2 tablespoons oil in heavy large nonstick skillet over high heat until hot. Add half of shrimp and sauté until cooked through, about 3 minutes. Using tongs, transfer shrimp to plate. Add 1 tablespoon oil to same skillet. Add remaining shrimp and sauté until cooked through, about 3 minutes. Transfer shrimp to plate and cool.

Cook corn in pot of boiling salted water until almost tender, about 5 minutes. Drain and cool. Cut corn kernels off cobs. Mix corn, tomatoes, and cucumber into shrimp.

Whisk remaining 2 tablespoons oil, ⅛ teaspoon pepper, lime juice, soy sauce, and sesame oil in medium bowl. (*Shrimp mixture and dressing can be made 4 hours ahead. Cover separately and refrigerate.*)

Combine shrimp mixture with any accumulated juices, avocado, greens, and mint in large bowl. Add dressing and toss to coat.

6 SERVINGS

Fireside Supper for 2

Caviar and Toast Points

Vodka on Ice

Baked Halibut with Orzo, Spinach, and Cherry Tomatoes
(opposite; pictured opposite)

Salad of Mixed Baby Greens

Chablis

Chocolate-Orange Pots de Crème with Candied Orange Peel
(page 214)

Shrimp Curry with Yu Choy and Kabocha Squash

1 pound yu choy, bottom 2 inches trimmed, stalks and leaves cut into 1½-inch-wide strips

4 cups ¾-inch cubes peeled seeded kabocha squash (from about one 2¾-pound squash)

2 13- to 14-ounce cans unsweetened coconut milk, divided

⅔ cup (packed) Thai basil leaves, divided

6 large fresh cilantro sprigs

3 double-leaf kaffir lime leaves,* chopped

1 tablespoon vegetable oil

1 large shallot, finely chopped

2 teaspoons Thai green curry paste*

1½ tablespoons minced lemongrass*

2½ tablespoons fish sauce (such as nam pla or nuoc nam)*

1 tablespoon golden brown sugar

¾ pound uncooked medium-size shrimp, peeled, deveined

Among the most nutritious Asian greens, *yu choy* is also one of the most beautiful to cook with, its tapering green leaves punctuated with bright yellow flowers. Western gardeners grew it as an ornamental until discovering its culinary potential, but Asian cooks have been using it as a vegetable since ancient times. The mildly bitter flavor of *yu choy* plays nicely against the sweet curry sauce and kabocha squash. Chinese broccoli or broccoli rabe (rapini) can be used instead. Serve with white rice.

Bring large saucepan of water to boil. Add yu choy. Cook until crisp-tender, about 1 minute. Using strainer, transfer yu choy to colander. Rinse with cold water and set aside. Return water to boil. Add squash. Boil until almost tender, about 4 minutes. Drain, rinse with cold water, and set squash aside.

Blend ½ cup coconut milk, ⅓ cup Thai basil leaves, cilantro, and lime leaves in mini processor or blender until herbs are finely chopped and loose paste forms.

Heat oil in large nonstick skillet over medium-high heat. Add shallot and curry paste; stir 30 seconds. Add herb paste and lemongrass; stir 1 minute. Add remaining coconut milk, fish sauce, sugar, and squash. Boil until squash is tender, about 4 minutes. Add shrimp and yu choy. Simmer until shrimp are opaque in center, about 2 minutes. Mix in ⅓ cup basil leaves. Season with salt and pepper and serve.

Available in the Asian foods section of many supermarkets, at some specialty foods stores, and at Asian markets.

4 SERVINGS

Oven-Roasted Dungeness Crab

  ¼ cup (½ stick) butter

  ¼ cup olive oil

   2 tablespoons minced garlic

   1 tablespoon minced shallot

1½ teaspoons dried crushed red pepper

   2 large Dungeness crabs, cooked, cleaned, and cracked (about 4¼ pounds)

   2 tablespoons chopped fresh thyme, divided

   2 tablespoons chopped fresh parsley, divided

  ½ cup blood orange juice or regular orange juice

   1 teaspoon finely grated blood orange peel or regular orange peel

Preheat oven to 500°F. Melt butter with oil in heavy large ovenproof skillet over medium-high heat. Stir in garlic, shallot, and dried crushed red pepper. Add crabs; sprinkle with salt and pepper. Sprinkle 1 tablespoon chopped thyme and 1 tablespoon chopped parsley over crabs. Stir to combine. Place skillet in oven and roast crabs until heated through, stirring once, about 12 minutes.

Using tongs, transfer crabs to platter. Add orange juice and peel to same skillet; boil until sauce is reduced by about half, about 5 minutes. Spoon sauce over crabs. Sprinkle with remaining 1 tablespoon thyme and 1 tablespoon parsley and serve.

2 SERVINGS

The buttery sauce that coats the crabmeat and the shells is part of the pleasure of this dish; to really enjoy it, dispense with the utensils and just eat the crab with your hands. Serve with a green salad dressed with tarragon vinaigrette and plenty of crusty sourdough bread.

Scallops with Hazelnuts and Browned Butter Vinaigrette

5	tablespoons unsalted butter
12	large sea scallops (about 1 pound)
1½	teaspoons chopped fresh thyme, divided
⅓	cup chopped shallots
¼	cup husked hazelnuts, toasted, chopped
1	tablespoon white balsamic vinegar
1	small bunch watercress, thick stems trimmed

Husked, chopped hazelnuts are available at many supermarkets.

Cook butter in large nonstick skillet over medium heat until deep golden brown and most of foam subsides, stirring often, about 4 minutes. Transfer butter to bowl. Sprinkle scallops with salt, pepper, and ½ teaspoon thyme. Add to skillet; cook until just opaque in center, about 1½ minutes per side. Transfer to plate. Add shallots, nuts, and 1 teaspoon thyme to skillet; stir 30 seconds. Remove skillet from heat. Mix in browned butter and white balsamic vinegar. Season with salt and pepper.

Divide watercress between plates. Top with scallops; spoon vinaigrette over.

2 SERVINGS

Farro Salad with Peas, Asparagus, and Feta

1½ cups semi-pearled farro

12 ounces asparagus, trimmed, cut into 1½-inch lengths

1 8-ounce package sugar snap peas

12 ounces grape tomatoes, halved

½ cup chopped red onion

6 tablespoons chopped fresh dill

½ cup olive oil

¼ cup Sherry wine vinegar

1 7-ounce package feta cheese, crumbled

Cook farro in large saucepan of boiling salted water until just tender, about 10 minutes. Drain. Transfer to large bowl.

Meanwhile, cook asparagus and sugar snap peas in another saucepan of boiling salted water until crisp-tender, about 3 minutes. Drain. Add to farro with tomatoes, onion, and dill. Whisk oil and vinegar in small bowl. Season dressing with salt and pepper. Add dressing and feta to salad; toss to coat and serve.

Farro is a grain with a mellow, nutty flavor. It is available in some supermarkets, specialty foods stores, and Italian markets.

4 SERVINGS

Grilled Portobello Mushroom Sandwiches with Red Pepper Mayonnaise

RED PEPPER MAYONNAISE

- 10 pitted Kalamata olives
- ¼ cup chopped drained roasted red peppers from jar
- 2 tablespoons chopped fresh basil
- 1 cup mayonnaise

SANDWICHES

- 1 cup balsamic vinegar
- 2 tablespoons Dijon mustard
- 2 tablespoons chopped fresh basil
- 2 tablespoons chopped fresh oregano
- 2 green onions, cut into 3-inch pieces
- 1 garlic clove, chopped
- ½ cup olive oil
- 6 4- to 5-inch-diameter portobello mushrooms, stemmed

- 6 slices mozzarella cheese
- 12 5x3x½-inch slices country-style bread

- 6 thin red onion slices
- 6 thick tomato slices
- 6 green lettuce leaves

FOR RED PEPPER MAYONNAISE: Place olives, red peppers, and basil in mini food processor. Puree until coarse paste forms. Transfer mixture to small bowl. Stir in mayonnaise. (*Can be made 2 days ahead. Cover and chill.*)

FOR SANDWICHES: Mix first 6 ingredients in blender until smooth. With blender running, gradually add oil. Place mushrooms in large resealable plastic bag. Add marinade; let mushrooms marinate at room temperature 30 minutes.

Prepare barbecue (medium-high heat). Drain mushrooms. Grill until soft and slightly charred, about 3 minutes per side. Transfer to plate. Place 1 slice cheese atop each hot mushroom. Grill bread until toasted, watching closely to prevent burning, about 1 minute per side.

Place toasted bread on work surface. Spread mayonnaise over each bread slice. Top 6 bread slices with 1 mushroom, then onion, tomato, and lettuce. Top with remaining bread. Cut in half.

MAKES 6

Post-Hike Lunch for 6

Grilled Portobello Mushroom
Sandwiches with
Red Pepper Mayonnaise
(at left)

Frisée Salad

Lemonade and *Iced Tea*

Cornmeal and Fig Cake with
Pine Nuts
(page 201)

Coffee

Butternut Squash, Rosemary, and Blue Cheese Risotto

   7 cups (or more) vegetable broth

   3 tablespoons butter

1¼ cups finely chopped onion

   1 2-pound butternut squash, peeled, halved, seeded, cut into ½- to ¾-inch dice (about 3 cups)

   2 teaspoons chopped fresh rosemary, divided

   2 cups arborio rice (about 13½ ounces)

 ½ cup dry white wine

   4 cups (packed) baby spinach leaves (about 4 ounces)

 ½ cup whipping cream

 ½ cup freshly grated Parmesan cheese

 ⅓ cup crumbled blue cheese (about 1½ ounces)

Bring 7 cups broth to boil in large saucepan. Cover and reduce heat to low.

   Melt butter in heavy large pot over medium heat. Add onion and sauté until tender, about 5 minutes. Add squash and 1½ teaspoons rosemary; sauté 4 minutes to coat with butter. Add rice and stir 2 minutes. Add wine and simmer until evaporated, about 1 minute. Add 7 cups hot broth; bring to boil. Reduce heat and simmer uncovered until rice is just tender and risotto is creamy and slightly soupy, adding more broth by ¼ cupfuls as needed to maintain consistency and stirring occasionally, about 18 minutes. Stir in spinach, cream, and Parmesan. Season with salt and pepper.

Transfer risotto to large bowl. Sprinkle with blue cheese and remaining ½ teaspoon rosemary and serve.

4 SERVINGS

Warm Lentils with Spinach and Goat Cheese

1	tablespoon olive oil
1	cup finely chopped onion
⅓	cup finely chopped celery
⅓	cup finely chopped carrot
2	bay leaves
12	ounces French green lentils
4	cups vegetable broth
⅓	cup mascarpone cheese*
1	tablespoon butter
1	pound fresh spinach leaves
1	5-ounce log soft fresh goat cheese, crumbled

Heat oil in large saucepan over medium-high heat. Add onion, celery, carrot, and bay leaves and sauté until light golden, about 7 minutes. Add lentils; stir 1 minute. Add vegetable broth; bring to boil. Cover, reduce heat to medium-low, and simmer until lentils are tender and nearly all liquid is absorbed, about 30 minutes. Discard bay leaves. Season to taste with salt and pepper. Stir in mascarpone cheese. (*Can be made 1 day ahead. Cover and refrigerate. Rewarm before continuing.*)

Melt butter in large pot over medium-high heat. Add spinach and cook until just wilted, stirring frequently.

Transfer lentils to large shallow serving bowl. Top with spinach, then crumbled goat cheese and serve.

*Italian cream cheese; available at many supermarkets and Italian markets.

6 SERVINGS

Dinner in the Kitchen for 4

Roasted Red Pepper and Feta Dip
(*page 20*)

Butternut Squash, Rosemary, and Blue Cheese Risotto
(*opposite; pictured opposite*)

Celery and Belgian Endive Salad
(*page 150*)

Pinot Grigio

Baked Apples Stuffed with Honey, Almonds, and Ginger
(*page 187*)

Sweet Potato Noodle Stir-Fry with Choy Sum and Shiitake Mushrooms

3 tablespoons sesame seeds

¼ cup Asian sesame oil

¼ cup mirin (sweet Japanese rice wine)*

3 tablespoons soy sauce

3 tablespoons (packed) golden brown sugar

2 tablespoons oyster sauce*

10 green onions, chopped

6 ounces fresh shiitake mushrooms, stemmed, caps cut into ⅓-inch-thick slices

1 pound choy sum or baby bok choy, just enough of bottoms cut off to separate stalks; stalks and leaves cut crosswise into 2-inch-wide strips

¼ pound snow peas (strings removed), cut in half lengthwise

1 medium carrot, peeled, cut into matchstick-size strips (about 1 cup)

8 ounces Chinese vermicelli with sweet potato starch*

3 tablespoons vegetable oil, divided

3 large shallots, sliced into thin rounds, divided

Stir sesame seeds in heavy medium skillet over medium-low heat until lightly toasted, about 4 minutes. Transfer to small dish.

Mix next 5 ingredients in small bowl. Stir in green onions and 2 tablespoons toasted sesame seeds; season with salt and pepper. Transfer 3 tablespoons sauce to medium bowl and mix in mushrooms; marinate 15 minutes.

Blanch choy sum, snow peas, and carrot in large pot of boiling salted water 1 minute. Using strainer, transfer vegetables to colander. Rinse with cold water and set aside to drain. Return water to boil; add noodles. Cook until just tender but still slightly chewy, stirring often, about 4 minutes. Drain, rinse with cold water, and drain again. Using kitchen shears, cut noodles crosswise in several places. (*Sauce, mushrooms, vegetables, and noodles can be prepared 2 hours ahead. Let stand at room temperature.*)

Heat 1 tablespoon vegetable oil in heavy large nonstick skillet over medium-high heat. Add half of shallots; stir 30 seconds. Add mushroom mixture; sauté until tender, about 4 minutes. Scrape mushroom mixture into large bowl. Heat 2 tablespoons oil in same skillet over medium heat. Add remaining shallots and stir 30 seconds. Add remaining sauce and noodles. Simmer until noodles absorb almost all sauce, stirring often, about 5 minutes. Add mixture to bowl with mushrooms. Add choy sum, snow peas, and carrot; toss. Season with salt and pepper. Transfer to large shallow bowl. Top with 1 tablespoon sesame seeds.

Available in the Asian foods section of many supermarkets, at some specialty foods stores, and at Asian markets.

4 SERVINGS

Feta, Garbanzo Bean, and Eggplant Pita Sandwiches

2 tablespoons olive oil
1 pound Japanese eggplants, unpeeled, cut into ¾-inch cubes
1½ cups chopped onions
1 15½-ounce can garbanzo beans, drained, ½ cup juices reserved
1 tablespoon ground cumin
1 tablespoon fresh lemon juice
4 tablespoons chopped fresh mint, divided
5 tablespoons crumbled feta cheese, divided

3 pita bread rounds, warmed in oven or toasted

Heat oil in large nonstick skillet over medium-high heat. Add eggplant cubes and onions; sauté until soft and beginning to brown, about 9 minutes. Stir in garbanzo beans, cumin, and lemon juice. Sauté until heated through and flavors blend, adding enough garbanzo bean liquid by tablespoonfuls to moisten if mixture is dry, about 4 minutes. Stir in 3 tablespoons mint and 3 tablespoons feta cheese. Season generously with salt and pepper.

Cut pita breads crosswise in half. Spoon eggplant mixture into pita breads. Sprinkle filling with remaining mint and feta and serve.

MAKES 6 HALVES

Thai Tofu with Zucchini, Red Bell Pepper, and Lime

2 tablespoons peanut oil, divided
1 12-ounce package extra-firm tofu, drained, patted dry, cut into
    ½-inch cubes
1 pound yellow and/or green zucchini, cut into ½-inch cubes
1 large red bell pepper, diced
1 tablespoon minced peeled fresh ginger
1⅓ cups canned unsweetened coconut milk
3 tablespoons (or more) fresh lime juice
1½ tablespoons soy sauce
¾ teaspoon Thai red curry paste
½ cup sliced fresh basil, divided

Look for Thai red curry paste in the Asian foods section of some supermarkets and at Asian markets. Serve this with rice noodles or steamed rice.

Heat 1 tablespoon oil in large nonstick skillet over medium-high heat. Add tofu; sauté until golden, about 4 minutes. Transfer tofu to bowl. Add remaining 1 tablespoon oil, then zucchini and bell pepper to skillet; sauté until beginning to soften, about 4 minutes. Return tofu to skillet. Add ginger; stir 30 seconds. Add coconut milk, 3 tablespoons lime juice, soy sauce, and curry paste; stir to dissolve curry paste. Simmer until sauce thickens, about 6 minutes. Season with salt and more lime juice, if desired. Stir in half of basil. Sprinkle with remaining basil and serve.

4 SERVINGS

Oven-Dried Tomato Tart with Goat Cheese and Black Olives

5 tablespoons extra-virgin olive oil, divided
6 medium tomatoes or large romas, cored, halved crosswise, seeded
2 small garlic cloves, thinly slivered
2 tablespoons minced fresh thyme, divided

1 sheet frozen puff pastry (half of 17.3-ounce package), thawed

1 cup coarsely grated whole-milk mozzarella cheese
½ cup soft fresh goat cheese (about 4 ounces)
2 large eggs
¼ cup whipping cream
⅓ cup oil-cured black olives, pitted
2 tablespoons freshly grated Parmesan cheese

Preheat oven to 300°F. Line rimmed baking sheet with foil; brush foil with 1 tablespoon oil. Place tomato halves, cut side up, on baking sheet. Sprinkle garlic and 1 tablespoon thyme over tomatoes; drizzle ¼ cup oil over. Sprinkle lightly with salt and pepper. Bake until tomatoes begin to shrink and are slightly dried but still soft, about 2 hours. Cool tomatoes on sheet. (*Can be prepared 1 day ahead. Store in single layer in covered container in refrigerator.*)

Roll out pastry on lightly floured surface to 13-inch square. Transfer pastry to 9-inch-diameter tart pan with removable bottom, pressing pastry firmly onto bottom and sides of pan. Trim overhang to ¾ inch. Fold overhang in and press, pushing crust ¼ inch above pan. Pierce crust all over with fork; chill 30 minutes.

Position rack in center of oven and preheat to 375°F. Line pastry with foil; fill with dried beans or pie weights. Bake until crust is set, about 20 minutes. Remove foil and beans; bake until crust edges are golden, piercing with fork if crust bubbles, about 12 minutes longer. Cool crust 10 minutes. Reduce oven temperature to 350°F.

Meanwhile, using fork, mash mozzarella cheese, goat cheese, and remaining 1 tablespoon thyme together in medium bowl. Season with salt and pepper. Add eggs and cream and stir until mixture is well blended. Spread cheese filling evenly in crust. Arrange tomato halves in filling, cut side up. Place olives between tomatoes. Sprinkle Parmesan cheese evenly over top. Bake until filling is puffed and set, about 35 minutes. Cool 5 minutes. Push up pan bottom, releasing sides. Serve tart warm.

6 TO 8 SERVINGS

Drunken Noodles

2	14-ounce packages ¼-inch-wide flat rice noodles*
¼	cup vegetable oil
12	garlic cloves, chopped
¼	cup chopped fresh Thai chiles*
1½	pounds ground chicken
¼	cup fish sauce (nam pla or nuoc nam)*
¼	cup black soy sauce*
¼	cup Golden Mountain sauce* or light soy sauce
1	tablespoon sugar
4	large plum tomatoes, each cut into 6 wedges
4	Anaheim chiles or Italian frying peppers, or 2 green bell peppers (about 12 ounces total), cut into strips
½	cup fresh Thai basil leaves* or regular basil leaves

Cook noodles in large pot of boiling salted water until tender but still firm to bite, stirring frequently. Drain.

Meanwhile, heat oil in heavy large pot over medium-high heat. Add garlic and Thai chiles; sauté 30 seconds. Add chicken and next 4 ingredients and sauté until chicken is cooked through, about 4 minutes. Add noodles, tomatoes, and Anaheim chiles; toss to coat. Transfer to large platter, sprinkle with basil leaves, and serve.

Available in the Asian foods section or produce section of some supermarkets, and at Southeast Asian and some Asian markets.

6 SERVINGS

There isn't a drop of alcohol in this dish—the name refers to how much you'll want to drink to combat the heat. We suggest a nice cold beer or sparkling wine.

Orecchiette with Garbanzos, Tomatoes, Feta, and Mint

1	pound orecchiette (ear-shaped pasta)
1	pound Golden Grape or cherry tomatoes (scant 4 cups), halved
7	tablespoons extra-virgin olive oil, divided
⅓	cup chopped fresh mint plus sprigs for garnish
⅓	cup thinly sliced green onions
¼	cup chopped fresh cilantro plus sprigs for garnish
2	garlic cloves, minced
1	15½-ounce can garbanzo beans (chickpeas), drained, patted dry
6	ounces feta cheese, coarsely crumbled (about 1½ cups)

Cook pasta in large pot of boiling salted water until tender but still firm to bite, stirring occasionally. Drain.

Meanwhile, combine tomatoes, 6 tablespoons olive oil, chopped mint, green onions, chopped cilantro, and garlic in large bowl. Season to taste with salt.

Heat remaining 1 tablespoon olive oil in medium skillet over medium-high heat. Add garbanzo beans and sauté until lightly browned, about 5 minutes. Add garbanzo beans and pasta to tomato mixture in bowl; toss to coat. Add feta; toss briefly. Season to taste with salt and pepper. Garnish with mint and cilantro sprigs.

6 SERVINGS

Ricotta Gnocchi with Leeks and Fava Beans

1   15- to 16-ounce container whole-milk ricotta cheese or 15 ounces fresh whole-milk ricotta cheese

1   small leek (white and pale green parts only), halved lengthwise, thinly sliced crosswise

1   large egg
½   cup freshly grated Parmesan cheese, plus additional for serving
1   teaspoon salt
¼   teaspoon ground black pepper
⅛   teaspoon ground nutmeg
⅔   cup all purpose flour, plus additional for dredging

1   cup shelled fresh fava beans or frozen double-peeled, thawed

½   cup (1 stick) butter
12   fresh sage leaves

Set large strainer lined with double-layer damp cheesecloth over large bowl. Place ricotta in prepared strainer; cover with plastic; chill overnight. (If using fresh ricotta, skip this step.)

Cook leek in small pot of boiling salted water until tender, about 7 minutes. Drain. Rinse under cold water; drain. Using hands, squeeze leek dry.

Mix ricotta, leek, egg, ½ cup Parmesan, salt, pepper, and nutmeg in bowl. Stir in ⅔ cup flour. Cover and chill mixture at least 1 hour and up to 1 day.

Line rimmed baking sheet with parchment paper. Place flour for dredging in flat bowl. For each gnocchi, shape 1 tablespoon ricotta mixture into ball, then drop into bowl of flour, tossing to coat. Transfer gnocchi to baking sheet. (*Can be made 4 hours ahead. Cover with plastic wrap; chill.*)

If using fresh fava beans, blanch in small saucepan of boiling salted water for 2 minutes; transfer to bowl of ice water. Peel beans.

Melt butter in large nonstick skillet over medium heat. Add fava beans and sage leaves. Sauté until butter browns, favas are tender, and sage is crisp, about 5 minutes. Set aside.

Bring large pot of salted water to boil. Working in 2 batches, add gnocchi and cook until tender and cooked through, about 5 minutes. Using slotted spoon, transfer to skillet with fava beans; toss to coat. When all gnocchi have been added to skillet, toss over medium heat to warm. Serve with Parmesan.

4 SERVINGS

Farfalle with Wilted Frisée and Burst Tomatoes

3 tablespoons extra-virgin olive oil

1½ pints cherry tomatoes

2 large garlic cloves, minced

1 teaspoon grated lemon peel

¼ teaspoon dried crushed red pepper

2 large heads of frisée (about 1 pound), coarsely chopped

12 ounces farfalle (bow-tie pasta)

4 tablespoons (½ stick) unsalted butter, cut into ½-inch pieces

½ cup freshly grated Parmesan cheese

Heat oil in heavy large skillet over medium-high heat. Add tomatoes and cook, stirring frequently, until tomatoes begin to burst, about 8 minutes. Add garlic, lemon peel, and dried crushed red pepper; cook 2 minutes longer. Add frisée in batches and cook until wilted, about 3 minutes total. Season tomato-frisée mixture with salt and pepper.

Meanwhile, cook pasta in pot of boiling salted water until tender but still firm to bite, stirring occasionally. Drain, reserving 1 cup cooking liquid.

Add pasta to skillet with tomato-frisée mixture. Stir in butter. Add reserved pasta liquid by ¼ cupfuls if dry. Divide pasta among shallow bowls and serve, passing cheese separately.

4 SERVINGS

Castellane Pasta with Sausage, Peppers, Cherry Tomatoes, and Marjoram

1	tablespoon extra-virgin olive oil
1	pound hot Italian sausages, casings removed
2	red bell peppers, chopped (about 2 cups)
1	large onion, chopped (about 2 cups)
2½	teaspoons chopped fresh marjoram
2	12-ounce packages cherry tomatoes
12	ounces castellane (long oval shells) or fusilli pasta
5	ounces crumbled goat cheese

Heat oil in large nonstick skillet over medium-high heat. Add sausages; sauté until browned, breaking up with back of fork, about 5 minutes. Add peppers and onion; sauté until soft and onion is golden brown, about 13 minutes. Stir in marjoram, then tomatoes. Simmer until tomatoes soften and release their juices, crushing with back of fork, about 5 minutes. Season generously with salt and pepper.

Meanwhile, cook pasta in large pot of boiling salted water until just tender but still firm to bite. Drain.

Return pasta to pot. Add sausage mixture and goat cheese; stir to blend. Transfer pasta to plates and serve.

4 SERVINGS

Mid-Week Pasta Party for 4

Antipasto Platter

Castellane Pasta with Sausage, Peppers, Cherry Tomatoes, and Marjoram
(at left)

Burrata Cheese with Shaved Vegetable Salad
(page 146)

Sangiovese

Sweet Cherry Sorbetto
(page 223)

Butter Cookies

Seafood Pasta with Lemon-Saffron Herb Dressing

- 12 ounces campanelle (trumpet-shaped pasta) or macaroni
- ⅛ teaspoon crushed saffron threads
- 7 tablespoons fresh lemon juice, divided
- 6 tablespoons extra-virgin olive oil, divided

- ½ cup mayonnaise
- ½ cup sour cream
- ¼ cup thinly sliced green onions
- 2 tablespoons drained capers
- 2 tablespoons minced fresh tarragon plus sprigs for garnish
- 1 tablespoon minced fresh dill plus sprigs for garnish
- 1 teaspoon sugar
- 1 pound cooked medium shrimp
- 1 cup finely chopped celery
- ½ pound Dungeness crabmeat

- 2 large handfuls of arugula
- 2 small heads of butter lettuce
- Lemon wedges

Cook pasta in large pot of boiling salted water until tender but still firm to bite, stirring occasionally. Drain, reserving ½ cup cooking liquid. Place 3 tablespoons hot cooking liquid in medium bowl. Sprinkle saffron over and let stand at room temperature 5 minutes. Transfer pasta to large bowl. Drizzle pasta with 1 tablespoon lemon juice and 1 tablespoon oil; toss to

coat. Let stand at room temperature until cool, stirring occasionally.

Add 6 tablespoons lemon juice, 5 tablespoons oil, mayonnaise, and next 6 ingredients to bowl with saffron liquid. Whisk to combine. Season dressing with salt and pepper. Pour dressing over pasta. Add shrimp and celery; toss to coat. Add reserved pasta cooking liquid by tablespoonfuls if mixture is dry. Add crab; toss gently. Cover; chill at least 1 hour and up to 4 hours.

Line platter with arugula and butter lettuce. Spoon pasta over. Garnish with lemon wedges and tarragon and dill sprigs. Serve cold.

6 SERVINGS

Bucatini All'Amatriciana

3 tablespoons extra-virgin olive oil, divided

4 ounces guanciale or unsmoked bacon, sliced, cut into 1x¼-inch strips, divided

1 garlic clove, peeled

1 1-inch dried peperoncino or ¼ teaspoon dried crushed red pepper

1 cup finely chopped onion

2 tablespoons balsamic vinegar

1 pound cherry tomatoes, chopped (about 3 cups)

12 ounces bucatini or spaghetti

¾ cup freshly grated Pecorino Romano cheese or Parmesan cheese (about 2½ ounces)

This is named after the town of Amatrice, not too far from Rome, where the sauce has long been prepared using the few ingredients that were always available: sun-ripened tomatoes, *guanciale* (salt-cured pork jowl), and a touch of fiery *peperoncino* (dried hot chile).

Heat 1 tablespoon oil in heavy large skillet over medium heat. Add half of guanciale and sauté until crisp, about 5 minutes. Transfer guanciale to paper towels (do not clean skillet). Reserve for garnish.

Add 2 tablespoons oil to same skillet over medium-low heat. Add garlic and peperoncino; sauté until peperoncino darkens, about 2 minutes. Add onion and remaining guanciale; sauté until onion is translucent and fat has rendered from guanciale, about 10 minutes. Stir in vinegar; cook 1 minute. Add tomatoes; simmer 6 minutes. Season sauce with salt and pepper.

Meanwhile, cook pasta in large pot of boiling salted water until just tender but still firm to bite. Drain, reserving ½ cup pasta cooking liquid. Return pasta to same pot.

Add tomato sauce and cheese to pasta and toss, adding some of reserved pasta cooking liquid if dry. Season to taste with salt and pepper. Transfer pasta to bowl. Sprinkle with reserved guanciale and serve.

4 SERVINGS

Fettuccine with Artichokes, Parsley, and Parmesan Cheese

1 lemon, halved
3 large artichokes

6 tablespoons extra-virgin olive oil
2 garlic cloves, peeled
6 tablespoons dry white wine
3 tablespoons chopped fresh Italian parsley, divided

12 ounces fettuccine

¾ cup freshly grated Parmesan cheese (about 2½ ounces), divided

Fill large bowl with cold water. Squeeze juice from lemon halves into water; add lemon halves. Working with 1 artichoke at a time, cut off stem from artichoke. Using small knife, peel stem, then slice into ¼-inch-thick rounds. Drop stem slices into lemon water. Pull off leaves from artichoke and discard. Using spoon, scoop out choke. Thinly slice artichoke bottom. Drop artichoke slices into lemon water. Repeat with remaining artichokes.

Heat oil in heavy large skillet over medium heat. Add garlic; sauté 1 minute. Drain artichoke pieces; add to skillet. Sauté until artichokes are soft and beginning to turn golden, about 20 minutes. Add wine; reduce heat to medium-low, cover, and simmer 3 minutes. Stir in 1½ tablespoons parsley; simmer 1 minute. Discard garlic. Season sauce with salt and pepper.

Meanwhile, cook pasta in large pot of boiling salted water until just tender but still firm to bite, stirring occasionally. Drain pasta, reserving 1 cup pasta cooking liquid.

Return pasta to pot; add artichoke sauce and half of cheese and toss to blend, adding some of reserved pasta cooking liquid if dry. Season to taste with salt and pepper. Transfer to bowl. Sprinkle with remaining cheese and 1½ tablespoons parsley and serve.

4 SERVINGS

Farmers' Market Dinner for 4

Honeydew and Prosciutto with Greens and Mint Vinaigrette
(double recipe; page 19)

Fettuccine with Artichokes, Parsley, and Parmesan Cheese
(at left, pictured opposite)

Salad of Fresh Herbs and Greens with Fried Eggplant
(page 152)

Chardonnay

Mixed Berries with Whipped Cream

Antipasto Pasta

- 12 ounces linguine
- 3 tablespoons olive oil
- 4 large (5-inch-diameter) portobello mushrooms, stemmed, dark gills removed, caps sliced ¼ inch thick
- 6 ounces ⅛-inch-thick slices Genoa salami, cut into thin strips
- 1 cup sliced vegetables and 6 tablespoons marinade from 16-ounce jar antipasto salad with olives
- 2 cups grated Asiago cheese, divided
- 2 cups chopped fresh basil, divided

Cook pasta in large pot of boiling salted water until just tender but still firm to bite, stirring occasionally. Drain, reserving ½ cup pasta cooking liquid.

Heat oil in same pot over medium-high heat. Add mushrooms; sauté until tender and brown, about 6 minutes. Add salami; toss 30 seconds. Add pasta, ½ cup cooking liquid, sliced vegetables, reserved marinade, and 1½ cups cheese; toss until liquid thickens and coats pasta, about 3 minutes. Mix in 1½ cups basil. Season with pepper. Transfer to bowl. Sprinkle with ½ cup basil; serve with ½ cup cheese.

4 SERVINGS

Linguine with Clams and Fresh Herbs

- 8 ounces linguine
- 2 tablespoons olive oil
- 2 garlic cloves, chopped
- 2 6½-ounce cans chopped clams in juice
- 1 tablespoon chopped fresh basil
- 1 tablespoon chopped fresh tarragon
- 1 tablespoon chopped fresh parsley
- 18 small clams (such as Manila or tiny littleneck), scrubbed
- ¼ cup whipping cream

Cook pasta in large pot of boiling salted water until tender but still firm to bite, stirring occasionally. Drain pasta.

Meanwhile, heat oil in heavy large skillet over medium-high heat. Add garlic and sauté until fragrant, about 30 seconds. Add canned clams with juice, basil, tarragon, and parsley. Add fresh clams. Cover; reduce heat to medium and cook until clams open, about 6 minutes. Using tongs, transfer fresh clams to plate (discard any clams that do not open). Add cooked pasta and whipping cream to sauce in skillet. Toss over medium-high heat until sauce is thick enough to coat pasta, about 1 minute. Season pasta to taste with salt and pepper. Divide pasta between bowls. Top with fresh clams and serve.

2 SERVINGS

The size of clams can vary, so larger ones may take a minute or two longer to cook.

Spaghetti Carbonara with Zucchini

 5 tablespoons extra-virgin olive oil
 1 garlic clove, peeled
 1 pound medium zucchini, trimmed, cut into ¼-inch-thick rounds (about 3½ cups)

 2 large eggs, room temperature
 ¾ cup freshly grated Parmesan cheese (about 2½ ounces)
12 ounces spaghetti

 6 large fresh basil leaves, torn into pieces, divided

Carbonara is a legendary Roman pasta dish. Here's a version that includes sautéed zucchini. It's meat-free yet every bit as delicious as the egg-and-bacon original.

Heat oil in heavy large skillet over medium heat. Add garlic and sauté until pale golden, about 1 minute. Add zucchini and sauté until beginning to color, about 15 minutes. Remove from heat; discard garlic.

Meanwhile, whisk eggs and Parmesan in large bowl to blend. Cook pasta in large pot of boiling salted water until just tender but still firm to bite, stirring occasionally. Drain pasta; add to egg mixture and toss to coat (heat from pasta will cook eggs).

Add zucchini mixture and half of basil to pasta; stir gently to blend. Season to taste with salt and pepper. Sprinkle with remaining basil and serve.

4 SERVINGS

Rigatoni with Red Peppers, Wild Mushrooms, and Fontina

- 2 tablespoons olive oil
- 2 large red onions, halved lengthwise, cut crosswise into ⅓-inch-thick slices (about 6 cups)
- 1 pound assorted wild mushrooms (such as small portobello, oyster, chanterelle, and stemmed shiitake), cut into ⅓-inch-thick slices (about 10 cups)
- 2 large red bell peppers, cut lengthwise into ⅓-inch-thick strips (about 4 cups)

- 1 pound rigatoni

- 3 teaspoons chopped fresh marjoram
- 1½ cups grated Fontina cheese (about 6 ounces), divided

Heat oil in heavy large pot over high heat. Add onions and cook until soft and beginning to brown, stirring frequently, about 8 minutes. Reduce heat to medium-high. Add mushrooms and sauté until wilted, about 3 minutes. Add peppers and sauté until just soft, about 5 minutes longer.

Meanwhile, cook pasta in large pot of boiling salted water until tender but still firm to bite, stirring occasionally. Drain, reserving 1 cup cooking liquid.

Add reserved pasta cooking liquid and marjoram to mushroom mixture in pot and stir over medium-high heat, scraping up browned bits. Add drained pasta to mushroom sauce and toss to coat. Add 1 cup grated cheese; stir until melted. Transfer pasta to large bowl; sprinkle with remaining ½ cup cheese.

6 SERVINGS

Use an assortment of autumn's first wild mushrooms in this hearty vegetarian pasta.

Pasta with Anchovies, Currants, Fennel, and Pine Nuts

½   cup extra-virgin olive oil
8   anchovy fillets
1   large onion, very thinly sliced
1   large fresh fennel bulb, trimmed, halved, very thinly sliced
¼   teaspoon dried crushed red pepper
2   plum tomatoes, chopped
¼   cup pine nuts
¼   cup dried currants

¾   pound perciatelli (thick hollow spaghetti) or linguine

¼   teaspoon saffron threads
1   cup fresh breadcrumbs, toasted

This dish is a variation on a traditional Sicilian pasta made with sardines. Anchovies have replaced the sardines, but the flavors are still very authentic.

Heat oil in large skillet over medium heat. Add anchovies; mash with back of fork. Add onion, fennel, and red pepper. Sauté vegetables until tender, about 5 minutes. Add tomatoes, pine nuts, and currants. Reduce heat to low and cook 5 minutes to blend flavors; season with salt and pepper.

Meanwhile, cook pasta in large pot of boiling salted water until tender but still firm to bite.

Drain pasta, reserving 1 cup cooking liquid. Add saffron to reserved liquid and stir to dissolve. Return pasta and saffron water to pot. Add tomato mixture; toss over low heat until sauce coats pasta. Mix in breadcrumbs and transfer to bowl.

4 SERVINGS

Pasta with Arugula, Pecorino, and Black Pepper

6 ounces penne or bucatini
3 tablespoons extra-virgin olive oil
1 cup (packed) fresh arugula, torn into
     pieces
⅓ cup (packed) freshly grated Pecorino
     Romano cheese (about 1 ounce)
    Freshly ground black pepper

Fill large serving bowl with hot water to heat bowl; let stand while cooking pasta. Cook pasta in large pot of boiling salted water until just tender but still firm to bite, stirring occasionally. Drain pasta, reserving ½ cup pasta cooking liquid. Pour out hot water from serving bowl. Immediately add drained pasta and oil to bowl, then arugula and cheese and toss to coat. If dry, add some of reserved pasta cooking liquid by tablespoonfuls. Season with salt and freshly ground black pepper and serve.

2 SERVINGS

Grilled Zucchini and Eggplant Pizza with Tapenade and Fontina

DOUGH
1¼ cups warm water (105°F to 115°F)
1 envelope (¼ ounce) active dry yeast
   Generous pinch of sugar
3¼ to 3¾ cups all purpose flour, divided

1 tablespoon extra-virgin olive oil
2½ teaspoons coarse kosher salt

TOPPING
3 medium zucchini (about 1 pound total), trimmed, cut lengthwise into ¼-inch-thick slices
2 small eggplants (about 1½ pounds total), cut lengthwise into ¼-inch-thick slices
¾ cup (about) extra-virgin olive oil, divided

¾ cup purchased black-olive tapenade* (about 5½ ounces)
3 tablespoons minced fresh marjoram or fresh oregano

¾ teaspoon dried crushed red pepper
1½ cups (packed) coarsely grated Fontina cheese
1 cup freshly grated Pecorino Romano cheese
½ cup chopped fresh Italian parsley

Ultra-creamy Fontina cheese and a layer of black-olive tapenade give this an unctuous, satisfying quality that is usually missing from other veggie pizzas. Team with a dry rosé or a spicy Rhône-style red.

FOR DOUGH: Stir 1¼ cups warm water, yeast, and sugar in large bowl to blend. Let stand until yeast dissolves, about 10 minutes. Whisk in 1 cup flour; let stand in warm draft-free area until bubbling, about 30 minutes.

Stir oil and salt, then 2 cups flour into yeast mixture. Knead dough in bowl until almost smooth and beginning to pull away from sides, adding ¼ cup more flour to prevent sticking. Turn dough out onto floured surface; knead until smooth and elastic, adding more flour by tablespoonfuls as needed (dough should be slightly sticky), about 7 minutes. Place dough in lightly oiled large bowl; cover with plastic wrap. Let dough rise in warm draft-free area until doubled in volume, about 1½ hours.

MEANWHILE, FOR TOPPING: Prepare barbecue (medium heat). Arrange zucchini and eggplant slices on 2 large baking sheets. Brush vegetables with oil; sprinkle with salt and pepper. Grill until tender and golden brown, about 4 minutes per side. Transfer to platter.

If using charcoal barbecue, remove grate and arrange coals so that 1 side of grill is hot and 1 side is cooler (for gas barbecue, adjust burners accordingly).

Sprinkle 3 baking sheets with flour. Punch down dough. Divide dough into 3 equal pieces; roll out each piece on floured surface to 12x8-inch oval. Transfer to prepared baking sheets. Brush dough tops with oil. Place ovals, oiled side down, on hot side of grill rack and grill until bottoms are firm (watch closely to avoid burning), about 3 minutes. Turn crusts over; grill until dough is set, about 2 minutes. Transfer to baking sheets, grill mark side up.

Spread ¼ cup tapenade over each pizza; arrange grilled zucchini and eggplant slices over. Sprinkle each with 1 tablespoon marjoram and ¼ teaspoon crushed red pepper. Drizzle lightly with oil. Sprinkle each with ½ cup Fontina and ⅓ cup Pecorino Romano. Return pizzas to cooler side of grill. Cover and grill until cheese melts, about 5 minutes. Sprinkle pizzas with parsley; slice and serve.

A thick paste or spread made from brine-cured olives, capers, anchovies, and seasonings; available at some supermarkets, specialty foods stores, and Italian markets.

MAKES 3 MEDIUM PIZZAS

Sausage, Red Onion, and Wild Mushroom Pizza

1	16-ounce ball purchased fresh pizza dough or 2 10-ounce purchased fully baked thin pizza crusts (such as Boboli)
⅔	cup finely grated Piave or Parmesan cheese
2¼	teaspoons finely chopped fresh rosemary, divided
½	teaspoon dried crushed red pepper
	Coarse kosher salt
1½	tablespoons olive oil, divided
2½	hot Italian sausages, casings removed
1	small red onion, thinly sliced
7	ounces fresh wild mushrooms (such as stemmed shiitake, oyster, and chanterelle), thickly sliced
1¾	cups coarsely grated whole-milk mozzarella cheese (about 7 ounces), divided
	Chopped fresh parsley (optional)

Position 1 rack in top third and 1 rack in bottom third of oven and preheat to 450°F. Lightly flour 2 baking sheets. Place dough on work surface; let stand until room temperature, about 20 minutes. Divide dough in half. Press and stretch each piece out on lightly floured surface to 5-inch round. Sprinkle each with ⅓ cup Piave cheese, ¾ teaspoon rosemary, and ¼ teaspoon crushed red pepper; sprinkle with coarse salt. Roll each piece of dough out to 10-inch round, pressing in seasonings. Transfer dough rounds to prepared baking sheets.

Heat 1 tablespoon oil in large nonstick skillet over medium-high heat. Add sausage. Sauté until brown, breaking into ½-inch pieces with back of spoon, about 5 minutes. Using slotted spoon, transfer to bowl. Add onion to skillet. Sauté until crisp-tender, about 2 minutes; transfer to plate. Add ½ tablespoon oil to skillet. Add mushrooms and ¾ teaspoon rosemary; sprinkle with salt and pepper. Sauté until brown, about 5 minutes. Leaving ½-inch plain border, top each dough round with ¾ cup mozzarella, then onion, sausage, and mushrooms.

Bake until crust bottoms are crisp, reversing sheets after 10 minutes, about 20 minutes total. Using large spatula, transfer to work surface. Sprinkle each with 2 tablespoons mozzarella, then parsley, if desired.

MAKES 2 PIZZAS

**Friday Night
Pizza Party for 4**

Olives, Peperoncini, and
Breadsticks

Sausage, Red Onion, and
Wild Mushroom Pizza
(at left, pictured opposite)

Radicchio and Romaine Salad

Chianti

Zabaglione Gelato
(page 224)

Red Pepper, Spinach, and Goat Cheese Pizza

1   10-ounce purchased fully baked thin pizza
      crust (such as Boboli)
¼   cup olive oil
3   garlic cloves, minced
3   cups (packed) baby spinach leaves
1½   cups thickly sliced mushrooms (5 to 6 ounces)
½   cup drained roasted red peppers from jar, cut
      into thin strips
½   cup paper-thin red onion slices
8   large fresh basil leaves, cut into thin strips
1   5-ounce package soft fresh goat cheese,
      coarsely crumbled

Preheat oven to 425°F. Place pizza crust on large
baking sheet. Mix oil and garlic in small bowl. Using pastry brush, brush 2 tablespoons oil
over crust. Top with spinach, then sprinkle with sliced mushrooms, peppers, onion, basil,
and cheese. Drizzle with remaining garlic oil.

Bake until crust is crisp, about 18 minutes. Transfer to board. Cut into wedges.

4 SERVINGS

Ciabatta Pizza with Gorgonzola, Walnut Pesto, and Pears

2   cups walnuts
1   cup olive oil
¼   cup honey
2   tablespoons chopped fresh thyme

1   loaf ciabatta bread (about 1⅓ pounds), halved horizontally
10   ounces thinly sliced Havarti cheese
6   ounces thinly sliced prosciutto, cut crosswise into strips
2   pears, halved, cored, thinly sliced
⅔   cup crumbled Gorgonzola cheese
2   cups arugula

Preheat oven to 450°F. Toast nuts on baking sheet until brown, about 6 minutes. Maintain
oven temperature. Transfer hot nuts to processor. Add oil, honey, and thyme; blend until
nuts are finely chopped. Season pesto to taste with salt and pepper.

Place bread halves, cut side up, on baking sheet. Spread pesto over bread, about 1 cup
per side. Top with Havarti. Bake until bubbly and golden, about 12 minutes. Top with prosciutto, then pears and Gorgonzola. Tuck in arugula. Sprinkle with pepper.

6 SERVINGS

Baby Roma Tomato and Onion Pizza with Rosemary

Fresh Pizza Dough (3 dough balls; see recipe)

16 baby Roma (plum) or cherry tomatoes, sliced ¼ inch thick
3 small onions, thinly sliced
2 tablespoons fresh rosemary leaves
6 tablespoons extra-virgin olive oil

Preheat oven to 450°F. Sprinkle 3 large rimless baking sheets with flour. Roll out each dough ball on lightly floured surface to 12-inch round. Transfer 1 round to each prepared sheet.

Scatter tomatoes, onions, and rosemary on each dough round. Drizzle each with 2 tablespoons oil and sprinkle with salt and pepper.

Bake pizzas until crusts are brown at edges and crisp on bottom, about 15 minutes. Transfer to work surface. Cut into wedges.

MAKES THREE 12-INCH PIZZAS

Fresh Pizza Dough

1½ cups warm water (105°F to 115°F)
1½ tablespoons sugar
1½ envelopes dry yeast
¼ cup olive oil
2½ teaspoons salt
4½ cups (or more) all purpose flour

Combine 1½ cups warm water and sugar in medium bowl. Sprinkle yeast over. Let stand until mixture is foamy, about 10 minutes; add oil and salt. Mound 4½ cups flour on work surface (or use large bowl). Make well in center and pour yeast mixture into well. Gradually mix flour into yeast mixture, kneading until dough forms. Continue to knead until dough is smooth and elastic, sprinkling with more flour by tablespoonfuls if dough is very sticky, about 8 minutes.

Oil large bowl. Add dough and turn to coat. Cover bowl with plastic wrap, then towel. Let rise in warm draft-free area until doubled in volume, about 1 hour. Punch dough down; knead gently until smooth. Shape into 3 balls.

MAKES 3 12-INCH PIZZA CRUSTS

Braised Baby Onions with Orange Juice
and Balsamic Vinegar (page 139)

On the Side

Side Dishes

Salads

Breads

Crushed Heirloom Potatoes

2 pounds unpeeled whole heirloom potatoes

3 ounces crumbled Gorgonzola cheese

½ cup pecans, toasted, chopped

¼ cup extra-virgin olive oil

2 cups (packed) baby arugula

Place potatoes in large pot. Pour enough cold water over to cover; salt generously. Bring to boil. Reduce heat and simmer until potatoes are just tender, 20 to 40 minutes (depending on variety). Drain. Return potatoes to pot. Using large wooden spoon, coarsely crush potatoes in pot. Add cheese, nuts, and oil. Stir in arugula and toss to blend. Season to taste with salt and pepper. Transfer to bowl and serve.

6 TO 8 SERVINGS

Roasted Balsamic Radicchio

2 large heads of radicchio (about 1 pound total), halved through core end, each half cut into 3 wedges with some core still attached

3 tablespoons olive oil

1 tablespoon chopped fresh thyme

Balsamic vinegar (for drizzling)

Preheat oven to 450°F. Rinse radicchio wedges in cold water; gently shake off excess water (do not dry completely). Place radicchio in large bowl. Drizzle with olive oil and sprinkle with thyme, salt, and pepper; toss to coat.

Arrange radicchio wedges, 1 cut side up, on rimmed baking sheet. Roast until wilted, about 12 minutes. Turn over and roast until tender, about 8 minutes longer.

Arrange radicchio on platter; drizzle with vinegar and serve.

4 SERVINGS

Radicchio (red-leaf Italian chicory) is available in many varieties. The most widely distributed in this country are the round head variety (*di Castelfranco or di Chioggia*), traditionally used in salads, and the long, flat, finger-shaped radicchio di Treviso, which is excellent grilled. Because the vinegar is simply drizzled over the radicchio at the end of this recipe try to find an artisan-quality balsamic, such as one labeled *condimento*, if not a premium *balsamico tradizionale*. Radicchio is also good when grilled on a barbecue or in a stovetop grill pan. Oil the grill or grill pan and cook until wilted and slightly charred, turning occasionally, about 5 minutes.

Corn on the Cob with Lime-Chive Butter

½ cup (1 stick) unsalted butter, room
   temperature
⅓ cup finely chopped fresh chives
2 teaspoons fresh lime juice
1 teaspoon finely grated lime peel
½ teaspoon fine sea salt
¼ teaspoon Hungarian sweet paprika
   Pinch of cayenne pepper

   Sugar (optional)
8 ears of corn

Mix first 7 ingredients in medium bowl. *(Can be made 2 days ahead. Cover and chill. Bring to room temperature before using.)*

TO BOIL CORN: Bring large pot of water to boil; add pinch of sugar, if desired. Husk corn. Add corn to pot. Return water to boil and cook corn 4 minutes. Drain corn and serve immediately with lime-chive butter.

TO GRILL CORN: Prepare barbecue (medium-high heat). Remove all but the innermost husks from corn. Fold back inner husks and remove corn silk. Rewrap inner husks around corn. Grill until husks are slightly charred and corn is tender, turning often, about 10 minutes. Serve immediately with lime-chive butter.

8 SERVINGS

Roasted Carrots, Parsnips, and Meyer Lemon

   Nonstick vegetable oil spray
1 pound large carrots (about 4), peeled, cut diagonally into ¼-inch-thick slices
1 pound large parsnips (about 5), peeled, cut diagonally into ⅛-inch-thick slices
20 large garlic cloves, peeled
1 Meyer lemon, halved lengthwise, cut crosswise into ⅛-inch-thick slices, seeds removed
6 tablespoons olive oil, divided
2 teaspoons coarse kosher salt, divided

2 tablespoons chopped fresh parsley

Spray 2 large rimmed baking sheets with nonstick spray. Position 1 rack in top third and 1 rack in bottom third of oven and preheat to 375°F. Combine carrots, parsnips, garlic, lemon slices, and 4 tablespoons oil in large bowl. Sprinkle with 1½ teaspoons salt and toss to coat evenly. Divide mixture between prepared sheets, spreading in single layer. Roast vegetables 20 minutes. Stir vegetables; reverse positions of sheets. Roast until vegetables are tender and brown at edges, about 20 minutes longer.

Transfer vegetables to platter. Drizzle with remaining 2 tablespoons oil; sprinkle with parsley. Season with pepper and ½ teaspoon salt. Serve warm or at room temperature.

6 SERVINGS

This side would be delicious with roasted chicken or broiled halibut.

Braised Baby Onions with Orange Juice and Balsamic Vinegar

2   pounds fresh small cipolline onions or pearl onions

¼   cup extra-virgin olive oil

¾   cup fresh orange juice

¾   cup balsamic vinegar

Blanch onions in large pot of boiling salted water 15 seconds. Using slotted spoon, transfer to large bowl of ice water to cool. Trim root end if necessary, leaving core intact. Peel onions.

Heat oil in large nonstick skillet over high heat. Add onions and sauté until onions have deep golden brown spots, about 9 minutes. Add orange juice and vinegar; bring to boil, scraping up browned bits. Reduce heat to medium-low, cover, and simmer until onions are just tender when pierced with knife, about 8 minutes. Using slotted spoon, transfer onions to medium bowl. Boil juices in skillet until syrupy and reduced to ⅔ cup, about 3 minutes. Pour over onions. Serve warm or at room temperature. (*Can be made 1 day ahead. Cover and chill. Rewarm or bring to room temperature before serving.*)

6 TO 8 SERVINGS

Cipolline onions are small, flat Italian onions. They can be found in the produce section of many supermarkets and Italian markets. The sweet sharpness of both the orange juice and the balsamic vinegar combines with the natural sugars in the onions to create a delicious dish that's perfect with roasted meats.

Pea Tendrils with Crimini Mushrooms and Leeks

    3 tablespoons butter
    1 cup thinly sliced leek (white and pale green parts only; about 1 medium)
    2 garlic cloves, minced
    8 ounces crimini mushrooms, sliced
    8 cups pea tendrils, left intact

Melt butter in large nonstick skillet over medium-low heat. Add leek; cover and cook until leek is soft but not brown, stirring often, about 7 minutes. Increase heat to medium-high; add garlic and mushrooms and sauté until mushrooms begin to brown, about 7 minutes. Add pea tendrils; cook until pea tendrils just begin to wilt, tossing often, about 3 minutes. Season with salt and pepper.

4 SERVINGS

White Beans with Tomatoes and Spinach

    1 10-ounce bag fresh spinach leaves

    3 tablespoons olive oil, divided
    1 cup sliced shallots (about 4 large)
   24 grape tomatoes or cherry tomatoes
    2 teaspoons minced fresh rosemary
    1 cup low-salt chicken broth
    3 15-ounce cans cannellini (white kidney beans), drained

Heat large deep nonstick skillet over high heat. Add spinach to dry skillet; toss until just wilted, about 3 minutes. Transfer to strainer set over bowl.

Heat 2 tablespoons oil in same skillet over medium-high heat. Add shallots; sauté 5 minutes. Reduce heat to medium; add tomatoes and rosemary and sauté 1 minute. Add broth; cover and cook until tomatoes soften, stirring occasionally, about 4 minutes. Remove from heat. Crush tomatoes with potato masher. Stir in beans and 1 tablespoon oil. Bring to boil over medium-high heat. Reduce heat to medium-low; simmer uncovered until juices thicken, about 15 minutes. (*Can be made 2 hours ahead. Let beans and spinach stand at room temperature. Rewarm over low heat.*)

Stir spinach into beans. Season with salt and pepper.

6 SERVINGS

Wild Mushroom, Haricot Vert, and Shallot Sauté

 5 tablespoons butter, divided
 4 large shallots, halved, thinly sliced
 1 teaspoon chopped fresh thyme
 1¼ pounds fresh wild mushrooms (such as chanterelles, stemmed shiitake, and oyster), trimmed, thickly sliced
 ½ pound button mushrooms, thickly sliced
 ⅓ cup Madeira

 ¾ pound haricots verts or small slender green beans, trimmed

 3 tablespoons (about) low-salt chicken broth (optional)

Melt ¼ cup butter in large pot over high heat. Add shallots and thyme; sauté until shallots begin to brown, about 4 minutes. Add all mushrooms; sprinkle with salt and pepper. Sauté until juices evaporate, about 10 minutes. Add Madeira; toss until evaporated, about 1 minute. Set aside.

Cook haricots verts in medium pot of boiling salted water until crisp-tender, about 4 minutes. Drain. Let stand until ready to use, up to 2 hours.

Add remaining 1 tablespoon butter to mushrooms in pot. Add haricots verts. Toss over medium-high heat until butter melts and vegetables are heated through, adding broth by tablespoonfuls if mixture is dry, about 3 minutes. Season to taste with salt and pepper. Transfer vegetables to bowl and serve.

8 SERVINGS

Roasted Butternut Squash, Red Grapes, and Sage

 1 2¼-pound butternut squash, peeled, seeded, cut into 1½-inch pieces
 1½ cups seedless red grapes (about 8 ounces)
 1 medium onion, cut into 1-inch pieces
 1 tablespoon thinly sliced fresh sage leaves
 2 tablespoons extra-virgin olive oil
 2 tablespoons (¼ stick) unsalted butter, melted
 ¼ cup pine nuts, toasted

Preheat oven to 425°F. Combine butternut squash, grapes, onion, and sage in large bowl. Drizzle with oil and melted butter. Season generously with salt and pepper. Toss to coat. Spread out onto large rimmed baking sheet. Roast until squash and onion begin to brown, stirring occasionally, about 50 minutes. Transfer to platter, sprinkle with toasted pine nuts, and serve immediately.

4 TO 6 SERVINGS

Apple, Potato, and Onion Gratin

- 12 tablespoons (1½ sticks) butter, divided
- 2 pounds onions, sliced
- 2 tablespoons (packed) chopped fresh thyme
- 4 teaspoons fine sea salt, divided
- ⅔ cup water
- ⅔ cup white wine
- 4 teaspoons sugar

- 2½ pounds Yukon Gold, yellow Finn, or German Butterball potatoes, peeled, cut into ¼-inch-thick rounds
- 2 pounds tart apples (such as Granny Smith, Pippin, or Pink Lady), peeled, halved, cored, cut into ¼-inch-thick slices

Preheat oven to 400°F. Butter 13x9x2-inch glass or ceramic baking dish. Melt 6 tablespoons butter in large nonstick skillet over medium heat. Add onions, thyme, and 2 teaspoons salt; sauté until onions are translucent, about 10 minutes. Increase heat to medium-high; sauté until onions are tender and begin to color, about 8 minutes longer. Remove from heat. Add 6 tablespoons butter, ⅔ cup water, wine, and sugar to skillet; stir and swirl skillet to combine. Bring to boil. Cool onion mixture to lukewarm.

Combine potatoes, apples, remaining 2 teaspoons salt, and onion mixture in large bowl; toss gently to blend. Transfer to prepared baking dish, spreading evenly. Cover dish with parchment paper, then cover with foil, shiny side down. Bake gratin until potatoes are tender, about 55 minutes. Uncover; bake until top browns and juices bubble thickly, about 20 minutes longer. (*Can be made 6 hours ahead. Let stand uncovered at room temperature. Rewarm, loosely covered with foil, in 300°F oven for 20 minutes.*) Let gratin stand 15 minutes before serving.

8 SERVINGS

Spinach and Leek Gratin
with Roquefort Crumb Topping

5	tablespoons butter, divided
3½	tablespoons horseradish Dijon mustard, divided
2⅓	cups fresh breadcrumbs made from crustless French bread
1	cup crumbled Roquefort cheese
3	9-ounce bags spinach leaves
1	8-ounce leek, halved lengthwise, thinly sliced crosswise (about 3 cups)
¾	cup heavy whipping cream

Preheat oven to 400°F. Melt 3 tablespoons butter in medium skillet over medium-high heat. Mix in 2 tablespoons mustard, then breadcrumbs. Sauté breadcrumbs until golden, about 5 minutes. Cool briefly. Mix in Roquefort cheese.

Toss 1½ bags spinach in large nonstick pot over high heat until wilted, about 3 minutes. Transfer to sieve set over bowl. Repeat with remaining spinach. Press on spinach to drain.

Melt 2 tablespoons butter in same pot over medium-high heat. Add leek and sauté 4 minutes. Add cream, remaining 1½ tablespoons mustard, and spinach. Toss until thick and blended, about 2 minutes. Season with salt and pepper. Transfer to 7x11-inch baking dish. Top with breadcrumb mixture. Bake until bubbling, about 10 minutes.

8 SERVINGS

Green Beans Braised with Tomatoes and Basil

    3   tablespoons extra-virgin olive oil
    1   cup finely chopped white onion
    2   garlic cloves, minced
1½   pounds green beans, trimmed
    2   large plum tomatoes, finely chopped (about 1 cup)
    1   cup (packed) fresh basil leaves

Heat oil in large nonstick skillet over medium heat. Add onion and garlic and sauté until onion softens slightly, about 5 minutes. Add green beans, tomatoes, basil leaves, and ½ cup water. Cook until beans are crisp-tender, stirring and tossing occasionally, about 10 minutes. Season to taste with salt and pepper. Transfer to bowl and serve.

6 SERVINGS

Frisée and Morel Ragout with Prosciutto

    3   tablespoons unsalted butter
    7   ounces small fresh morel mushrooms
¼   cup minced shallots (about 2)
¾   cup low-salt chicken broth
    2   small heads of frisée (about 6 ounces), torn into 2-inch pieces
    1   cup fresh sweet peas or frozen petite peas, thawed
½   cup crème fraîche or whipping cream
    4   thin prosciutto slices (about 1 ounce), cut into thin strips
    2   teaspoons fresh lemon juice

Melt butter in large skillet over medium-high heat. Add mushrooms and sauté, stirring frequently, until juices are released, about 3 minutes. Add shallots; sauté 1 minute. Add broth; bring to simmer. Cover skillet and simmer until mushrooms are tender, about 5 minutes. Add frisée and stir until just wilted. Add peas and crème fraîche; bring to simmer. Stir in prosciutto and lemon juice. Season with salt and pepper.

4 TO 6 SERVINGS

Celebration Dinner for 8

Goat Cheese and Black Pepper Biscuits with Smoked Salmon and Dill
(page11)

Champagne

Prime Rib

Roasted Balsamic Radicchio
(double recipe; page137)

Spinach and Leek Gratin with Roquefort Crumb Topping
(opposite, pictured opposite)

Cabernet Sauvignon

Toffee Crunch Caramel Cheesecake
(page 196)

Cognac

Burrata Cheese with Shaved Vegetable Salad

- 2 heads of Belgian endive
- 2 celery stalks plus 1 cup pale green and yellow inner celery leaves (from about 1 large bunch)
- 1 fresh fennel bulb, trimmed
- 4 tablespoons Tuscan-style extra-virgin olive oil, divided
- 2 tablespoons fresh lemon juice

- 2 4-ounce rounds burrata cheese*
  Freshly ground black pepper

Using mandolin or V-slicer or large sharp knife, very thinly slice endive, celery stalks, and fennel bulb crosswise. Combine sliced vegetables and celery leaves in medium bowl. Add 3 tablespoons oil and lemon juice and toss to coat. Season salad with salt and ground black pepper.

Cut each burrata cheese round into 6 wedges or pieces. Divide salad among plates. Top each with 3 cheese wedges. Drizzle 1 tablespoon oil over cheese; sprinkle with pepper.

*Burrata, *a fresh cow's milk cheese, is sold at cheese shops and Italian markets.*

4 SERVINGS

Mixed Greens with Oranges, Watercress, and Onion

Saturday Night Dinner for 6

Broccoli Soup with
Chive-Cayenne Oil
(page 30)

Wine-Braised Leg of Lamb
with Garlic
(page 52)

Roasted Potatoes

Tomato, Cucumber, and
Green Pepper Chopped Salad
with Mint
(at left)

Zinfandel

Walnut Torte with
Coffee Whipped Cream
(page 209)

> 3 tablespoons white wine vinegar
> 1 tablespoon honey
> 1 teaspoon grated orange peel
> ½ cup olive oil
> 1 cup paper-thin slices white or red onion
>
> 3 oranges
> 1 5-ounce bag mixed baby greens
> 1 large bunch watercress, thick stems trimmed

Mix vinegar, honey, and orange peel in small bowl. Gradually whisk in oil. Season dressing with salt and pepper. Transfer 3 tablespoons dressing to medium bowl; mix in onion. Let stand at room temperature at least 1 hour and up to 3 hours, stirring occasionally.

Cut peel and white pith from oranges. Working over small bowl, cut between membranes to release orange segments. Combine mixed greens and watercress in large bowl. Drain orange segments; add to bowl with greens. Add onion with dressing. Toss, adding enough additional dressing to coat. Season salad to taste with salt and pepper. Divide among plates and serve.

6 SERVINGS

Tomato, Cucumber, and Green Pepper Chopped Salad with Mint

> 3 tablespoons fresh lemon juice
> 1 large garlic clove, minced
> 6 tablespoons olive oil
> 1 small head of romaine lettuce, cut into thin ribbons
> 12 ounces tomatoes, seeded, diced
> 1 12-ounce cucumber, peeled, seeded, diced
> 1 green bell pepper, diced
> 3 green onions, chopped
> 2 cups fresh whole mint leaves

Mix lemon juice and garlic in large bowl. Whisk in oil. Add remaining ingredients; toss. Season with salt and pepper.

6 SERVINGS

Avocado and Mango Salad with Passion Fruit Vinaigrette

    3 tablespoons frozen passion fruit juice concentrate, thawed
    3 tablespoons minced shallot
    4 teaspoons Sherry wine vinegar
    1 teaspoon Dijon mustard
    1 teaspoon whole coriander seeds, coarsely cracked
    3 tablespoons olive oil
    8 cups herb salad mix (about 4 ounces)
    1 large ripe mango, halved, pitted, peeled, sliced
    2 small avocados, halved, pitted, peeled, sliced

Whisk first 5 ingredients in small bowl to blend; gradually whisk in oil. Season dressing generously with salt and pepper. Toss salad mix in large bowl with ¼ cup dressing. Divide salad among 4 plates. Tuck mango and avocado into salad; drizzle some of remaining dressing over mango and avocado.

4 SERVINGS

Spring Greens with Sherry Vinaigrette

    ¼ cup Sherry wine vinegar
    2 teaspoons Dijon mustard
    2 teaspoons brown sugar
    ¼ cup extra-virgin olive oil

    4 cups mâche or baby spinach (about 2 ounces)
    4 cups arugula (about 2 ounces)
    ½ cup thinly sliced green onions

Whisk vinegar, mustard, and brown sugar in small bowl. Whisk in olive oil. Season dressing to taste with salt and pepper.

Mix mâche, arugula, and green onions in large bowl; toss with dressing and serve.

8 SERVINGS

Seafood Dinner for 4

Oysters on the Half Shell

Oven-Roasted Dungeness Crab
(double recipe; page 102)

Avocado and Mango Salad with
Passion Fruit Vinaigrette
(at left, pictured opposite)

Sourdough Bread

Pinot Gris

Meyer Lemon
Buttermilk Pudding Cake with
Fresh Berries
(page 199)

Celery and Belgian Endive Salad

3 garlic cloves, chopped
3 anchovy fillets, rinsed, patted dry
Large pinch of coarse kosher salt
¼ cup extra-virgin olive oil
1 tablespoon red wine vinegar
2 teaspoons Dijon mustard

4 large heads of Belgian endive
(about 1⅓ pounds), halved
lengthwise, then cut lengthwise
into thin strips
4 celery stalks (about ½ pound), cut
into 4-inch lengths, then cut
lengthwise into thin strips

Mix garlic, anchovies, and salt in small bowl. Mash with back of wooden spoon or firm spatula until paste forms. Whisk in oil, vinegar, and mustard. Season dressing to taste with salt and generously with pepper.

Place endive and celery in large bowl of ice water. Refrigerate 1 hour. Drain well. Place in clean bowl. Toss with anchovy dressing and serve.

4 SERVINGS

Butter Lettuce and Radicchio Salad with Strawberries

3 tablespoons tarragon vinegar
1 tablespoon sugar
2 teaspoons Dijon mustard
¼ teaspoon paprika
½ cup olive oil

1 large head of radicchio, torn into 1-inch pieces (about 6 cups)
1 head of butter lettuce, torn into 1-inch pieces (about 6 cups)
1 1-pint basket strawberries, hulled, halved
½ cup paper-thin red onion slices

Whisk vinegar, sugar, mustard, and paprika in small bowl to blend. Whisk in oil. Season dressing with salt and pepper.

Combine radicchio, butter lettuce, strawberries, and onion in large bowl. Toss with enough dressing to coat.

8 SERVINGS

Watermelon, Ricotta Salata, Basil, and Pine Nut Salad

- 3 tablespoons thinly sliced fresh basil
- 2 tablespoons fresh lime juice
- 2 tablespoons extra-virgin olive oil
- 1 4-pound seedless watermelon, cut into ½-inch cubes (about 6 cups)
- ½ pound ricotta salata (salted dry ricotta cheese),* cut into ¼-inch cubes
- ¼ cup pine nuts, toasted

Whisk first 3 ingredients in small bowl. Season dressing with salt and pepper. Place watermelon and ricotta salata in medium serving bowl. Drizzle with dressing; toss. Sprinkle with pine nuts.

Available at supermarkets, Italian markets, and specialty foods stores.

6 SERVINGS

Carrots in Cumin Dressing

- 2 tablespoons red wine vinegar
- 1 tablespoon fresh lemon juice
- 1 teaspoon ground cumin
- 1 teaspoon Hungarian sweet paprika
- ¼ teaspoon ground allspice
- 6 tablespoons olive oil

- 2½ pounds large carrots, peeled, cut on diagonal into ½-inch-thick ovals
- ¼ cup chopped fresh cilantro

Combine first 5 ingredients in small bowl; whisk in oil. Season dressing with salt and pepper. (*Can be made 1 day ahead. Cover and store at room temperature.*)

Cook carrots in pot of boiling salted water until crisp-tender, about 6 minutes. Drain; place in bowl. Mix in dressing. Let stand 30 minutes, tossing often. Season with salt and pepper. Mix in cilantro.

6 SERVINGS

Jicama, Radish, and Pepita Salad

½ cup olive oil
⅓ cup chopped fresh cilantro
1½ tablespoons white wine vinegar
1 tablespoon honey
1¼ teaspoons ground cumin

1 5-ounce package butter lettuce mix or baby spinach leaves
2 cups diced peeled jicama
1 scant cup thinly sliced radishes (about 8)
⅓ cup natural shelled pumpkin seeds (pepitas), lightly toasted
½ cup coarsely crumbled queso fresco or Cotija cheese

Whisk first 5 ingredients in small bowl. Season dressing with salt and pepper.

Toss lettuce, jicama, and radishes in large bowl. Add dressing and toss to coat. Divide salad among 4 plates. Sprinkle with pumpkin seeds and cheese and serve.

4 SERVINGS

Salad of Fresh Herbs and Greens with Fried Eggplant

1 small shallot, minced
2 tablespoons Champagne vinegar or fresh lemon juice
¼ teaspoon (or more) ground sumac* (optional)
¼ teaspoon ground cumin
7 tablespoons (or more) extra-virgin olive oil, divided
1½ cups (loosely packed) fresh Italian parsley leaves
1½ cups (loosely packed) arugula, torn if large
1 cup (loosely packed) small fresh basil leaves
1 cup (loosely packed) torn fresh sorrel or baby spinach leaves
1 cup (loosely packed) fresh mint leaves
⅓ cup (loosely packed) 1-inch pieces fresh chives
⅓ cup (loosely packed) fresh chervil leaves (optional)

2 10- to 12-ounce eggplants, stems cut off
Coarse kosher salt

Nasturtium blossoms or other edible flowers (optional)

Whisk shallot, vinegar, ¼ teaspoon sumac, and cumin in small bowl. Gradually whisk in 4 tablespoons oil. Season dressing with salt and pepper. Combine herbs and greens in large bowl. (*Dressing and salad can be made 2 hours ahead. Cover separately and chill.*)

Latin American Lunch for 4

Grilled Steak Sandwiches with
Chimichurri and Bell Peppers
(*page 40*)

Jicama, Radish, and
Pepita Salad
(*opposite*)

Iced Tea

Flan

Using vegetable peeler, remove eggplant peel in vertical strips every 1 to 1½ inches, making striped pattern. Cut eggplants crosswise into ⅓-inch-thick rounds. Place rounds in large colander. Sprinkle generously with kosher salt and toss to coat evenly. Let stand until rounds soften and release moisture, tossing occasionally, about 1 hour. Rinse rounds, 1 at a time, and press to release excess moisture. Arrange rounds in single layer on several thicknesses of paper towels. Pat dry with additional towels.

Heat remaining 3 tablespoons oil in large skillet over medium-high heat. Working in batches, fry eggplant until golden and soft, adding more oil by tablespoonfuls as needed, about 2 minutes per side. Transfer eggplant to paper towels to drain.

Overlap eggplant rounds on platter. Sprinkle with pepper and more sumac, if desired. Toss herbs and greens with dressing; season to taste with salt and pepper. Mound salad atop eggplant. Garnish with nasturtium blossoms, if desired, and serve.

A fruity and acidic seasoning powder made from ground dried sumac berries. It is available at Middle Eastern markets.

6 TO 8 SERVINGS

Grilled Panzanella Salad with Bell Peppers, Summer Squash, and Tomatoes

SALAD

1½ pounds assorted bell peppers (about 3 large), cut into 1½-inch-wide strips

1½ pounds assorted summer squash, cut lengthwise into ⅓-inch-thick slices

1 medium-size red onion, cut into ¼-inch-thick rounds

1 12- to 14-ounce loaf of ciabatta, some crust trimmed to expose bread, cut crosswise into 1-inch-thick slices

Extra-virgin olive oil

1 garlic clove, peeled, cut into thirds

DRESSING

¼ cup fresh lemon juice

2 tablespoons red wine vinegar

1 tablespoon grated lemon peel

⅓ cup extra-virgin olive oil

1 pound tomatoes, cored, cut into ¾-inch dice, juices reserved

½ cup chopped fresh Italian parsley

¼ cup coarsely chopped assorted fresh herbs (such as chives, dill, chervil, and tarragon)

2 tablespoons drained capers

FOR SALAD: Prepare barbecue (medium heat). Brush both sides of bell peppers, squash, onion, and bread slices lightly with olive oil; sprinkle with salt and pepper. Grill vegetables until tender and brown, about 4 minutes per side for peppers and squash and 3 minutes per side for onion. Grill bread until browned and crisp, turning occasionally, about 4 minutes. Cool slightly. Rub bread with cut sides of garlic. Tear bread into ¾-inch pieces; place in very large bowl. Cut grilled vegetables into 1-inch pieces; add to bread in bowl.

FOR DRESSING: Whisk first 3 ingredients in small bowl to blend. Gradually whisk in ⅓ cup oil. Season dressing with salt and pepper.

Add dressing, tomatoes with juices, and all remaining ingredients to salad; toss. Let stand 20 minutes. Season with salt and pepper.

8 SERVINGS

Chopped Honey-Mustard Slaw

    1 2-pound head of green cabbage, quartered, cored, thinly sliced
          lengthwise, then chopped crosswise (about 16 cups)
    1 tablespoon coarse kosher salt

    ¾ cup mayonnaise
  2½ tablespoons honey
    2 tablespoons Dijon mustard
  1½ teaspoons celery seeds
    1 teaspoon grated lemon peel
    ½ teaspoon hot pepper sauce

Place cabbage in large colander; set colander over large bowl. Sprinkle salt over cabbage and toss. Cover with plastic; chill overnight.

Whisk all remaining ingredients in small bowl to blend. (*Dressing can be prepared 1 day ahead. Cover and chill.*)

Discard all liquid accumulated in bowl from cabbage. Rinse cabbage under cold water to remove some of salt. Working in batches, squeeze out as much liquid as possible from cabbage. Transfer cabbage to large serving bowl. Pour ¾ cup dressing over and toss to coat. Cover and refrigerate at least 1 hour. (*Can be made 1 day ahead. Keep refrigerated.*) Season with pepper.

8 SERVINGS

Pool Party for 8

Crudites Platter

Strawberry and Peach Sangria
(*page 32*)

Mustard-Seed-Crusted Burgers
with Horseradish Slaw
(*double recipe; page 45*)

Chopped Honey-Mustard Slaw
(*at left*)

Lemonade, Iced Tea, and *Beer*

Watermelon

Honey-Roasted Pear Salad
with Thyme-Verjus Dressing

DRESSING

- ⅓ cup verjus or 3 tablespoons white grape juice and 2 tablespoons apple cider vinegar
- ⅓ cup grapeseed oil
- 1 large shallot, finely chopped
- 2 teaspoons fresh thyme leaves

PEARS AND SALAD

- 3 bunches fresh thyme sprigs
- 4 ripe but firm Bartlett pears (about 2½ pounds), halved, cored
- ¼ cup honey

- 1 head of butter lettuce, coarsely torn
- 4 ounces baby arugula
- 6 ounces blue cheese, sliced or coarsely crumbled
- ½ cup hazelnuts, toasted, coarsely chopped

FOR DRESSING: Whisk all ingredients in small bowl to blend. Season dressing to taste with salt and pepper.

FOR PEARS AND SALAD: Preheat oven to 400°F. Scatter thyme sprigs on rimmed baking sheet. Place pear halves, cut side down, on work surface. Starting ½ inch from stem and leaving pear half intact, cut each lengthwise into scant ⅓- to ½-inch-wide slices. Press pear gently to fan slices; place atop thyme sprigs. Drizzle pears with honey; sprinkle with salt and pepper. Bake until tender, about 15 minutes. Let stand on baking sheet at least 30 minutes and up to 3 hours.

Combine lettuce and arugula in large bowl. Add dressing and toss to coat. Divide salad among plates. Place pear alongside greens. Garnish salads with cheese; sprinkle with nuts.

8 SERVINGS

Verjus is a tart grape juice made from unripe wine grapes. Milder than vinegar, it can be used in salad dressings without competing with an accompanying wine the way vinegar does. Look for it at specialty foods stores. The salad is delicious with lamb chops and an Oregon Pinot Noir.

Radicchio and Endive Caesar with Ciabatta Crisps

- 2 tablespoons fresh lemon juice
- 2 teaspoons anchovy paste
- 2 teaspoons Dijon mustard
- ½ teaspoon Worcestershire sauce
- 1 garlic clove, pressed
- ½ cup plus 2 tablespoons olive oil
- ¾ cup freshly grated Parmesan cheese, divided

- 12 ⅓-inch-thick slices ciabatta

- 1 large head of radicchio, leaves torn into pieces
- 5 heads of Belgian endive, leaves separated
- 4 ounces Parmesan cheese shavings

Position rack in top third of oven and preheat to 450°F. Whisk lemon juice, anchovy paste, Dijon mustard, Worcestershire sauce, and pressed garlic in large bowl to blend. Whisk in ½ cup olive oil, then ¼ cup grated Parmesan cheese. Season to taste with salt and pepper.

Place ciabatta on baking sheet; brush with 2 tablespoons oil, then sprinkle with pepper and remaining ½ cup grated cheese. Bake until crisp, about 15 minutes.

Toss radicchio and endive with dressing in large bowl. Divide among plates. Top with cheese shavings. Serve with ciabatta crisps.

6 SERVINGS

Yukon Gold Potato Salad with Crispy Prosciutto and Truffle Oil

- 2 pounds Yukon Gold potatoes, peeled, cut into ¼-inch-thick slices
- 2½ cups low-salt chicken broth

- 2 tablespoons (¼ stick) butter
- 3 ounces chopped sliced prosciutto
- 1 cup chopped celery
- ½ cup chopped sweet onion (such as Vidalia or Maui)
- ½ cup chopped fresh chives
- 1 tablespoon (or more) truffle oil
- 1 tablespoon fresh lemon juice

Place potatoes in large saucepan. Add chicken broth. Bring to boil. Reduce heat to medium and simmer, partially covered, until potatoes are just tender, about 6 minutes. Drain potatoes, reserving broth. Place potatoes in large bowl. Return broth to same saucepan and boil

Steak Dinner for 4

Shrimp Cocktail

Chipotle-Rubbed Steaks with
Gorgonzola Toasts
(page 46)

Radicchio and Endive Caesar
with Ciabatta Crisps
(opposite)

Sautéed Zucchini

Zinfandel

Chocolate-Brandy
Bread Pudding with Cinnamon
Whipped Cream
(page 210)

until reduced to ⅔ cup, about 13 minutes. Pour over potatoes and toss gently until broth is absorbed.

Melt butter in medium nonstick skillet over medium heat. Add prosciutto and sauté until crisp, about 6 minutes. Transfer prosciutto and butter from skillet to bowl with potatoes. Add celery, onion, and chives to potatoes. Whisk 1 tablespoon truffle oil and lemon juice in small bowl to blend. Drizzle over potato mixture; toss to coat. Season salad to taste with salt, pepper, and additional truffle oil, if desired. Serve warm or at room temperature. *(Can be made 2 hours ahead. Let stand at room temperature.)*

6 SERVINGS

Warm Chestnut and Apple Salad

6 cups (packed) arugula

6 cups (packed) coarsely torn curly endive

3 tablespoons extra-virgin olive oil, divided

1½ medium Granny Smith apples, peeled, cored, cut into ½-inch dice

¾ cup thinly sliced shallots

1½ cups steamed chestnuts (from two 7.25-ounce jars), coarsely chopped

3 tablespoons red wine vinegar

4½ tablespoons walnut oil

Toss arugula and endive in large bowl. *(Can be prepared 6 hours ahead. Cover with damp kitchen towel; chill.)*

Heat 1½ tablespoons olive oil in large skillet over medium-high heat. Add apples and shallots; sauté 5 minutes. Add chestnuts; sauté 1 minute. Stir in vinegar, scraping up any browned bits. Remove from heat; stir in walnut oil and remaining 1½ tablespoons olive oil. Season with salt and pepper. Pour chestnut mixture over arugula mixture; toss. Divide salad among 8 plates.

8 SERVINGS

Pineapple, Cucumber, and Green Onion Salad

- ¼ cup unseasoned rice vinegar
- ¼ cup palm sugar or dark brown sugar
- 2 tablespoons minced peeled fresh ginger
- 2 red Thai chiles or red jalapeño chiles, halved, seeded, thinly sliced
- 1 teaspoon Asian sesame oil
- 4 cups ½-inch cubes peeled cored fresh pineapple (from 1 large)
- 2 cups ½-inch cubes peeled seeded cucumber (from 1 pound)
- 2 large green onions, chopped
- 2 tablespoons salted roasted peanuts

Whisk first 5 ingredients in large bowl to blend. Add pineapple, cucumber, and green onions; toss. Season with salt and pepper. *(Can be made 3 hours ahead. Cover; chill.)* Sprinkle with peanuts.

8 SERVINGS

South Seas Dinner for 8

Chicken Satays on Lemongrass Spears with Peanut Sauce
(page 14)

Passion Fruit-Pineapple Vodka Coolers
(page 37)

Coconut Beef Curry on Chinese Egg Noodles
(page 46)

Pineapple, Cucumber, and Green Onion Salad
(at left, pictured at left)

Stir-Fried Snow Peas

Alsatian Riesling

Banana Fritters with Coconut Ice Cream
(page 192)

Pecan Praline Trellis

DOUGH

3 tablespoons plus 2¼ cups (or more) unbleached all purpose flour

1½ teaspoons instant or rapid-rise yeast (measured from 1 envelope)

3 tablespoons warm water (105°F to 115°F)

½ cup plus 1 tablespoon sour cream

4½ tablespoons sugar

3 large egg yolks

1 tablespoon vanilla extract

¾ teaspoon salt

4½ tablespoons unsalted butter, cut into 4 pieces, room temperature

FILLING

1½ cups pecans (about 6 ounces)

1½ teaspoons vegetable oil

⅛ teaspoon fine sea salt

6 tablespoons (¾ stick) unsalted butter, room temperature

1½ cups golden brown sugar

1 egg, beaten to blend (for glaze)

FOR DOUGH: Mix 3 tablespoons flour and yeast in small bowl to blend. Add 3 tablespoons warm water; whisk until smooth. Let mixture stand until puffed, about 12 minutes.

Combine 2¼ cups flour, sour cream, sugar, egg yolks, vanilla, salt, and yeast mixture in large bowl of heavy-duty mixer fitted with paddle attachment. Beat on medium speed until dough is sticky, adding 1 to 2 tablespoons water if mixture is too dry, about 5 minutes. Add butter; beat until dough is smooth and soft, adding more flour by tablespoonfuls until dough is slightly firmer and pulls away from sides of bowl, about 5 minutes. Cover bowl with plastic wrap. Let dough rise in warm draft-free area until at least doubled in volume, about 2 hours.

MEANWHILE, PREPARE FILLING: Preheat oven to 400°F. Toss pecans and oil on rimmed baking sheet to coat. Bake until aromatic, about 5 minutes. Sprinkle nuts with ⅛ teaspoon sea salt; cool on sheet. Coarsely chop pecans.

Scrape dough out onto floured surface. Toss dough to coat with flour and press gently to deflate. Line work surface with long sheet of parchment paper; sprinkle paper with flour. Roll out dough on prepared parchment to 16x14-inch rectangle. Using offset spatula, spread butter lengthwise in 5 inch-wide strip down center of dough. Sprinkle sugar, then nuts over butter. Cut unfilled dough on either side of filling into ¾-inch-wide diagonal strips. Fold alternating strips over filling on slight diagonal, forming lattice top. Fold loose ends under bottom edge of bread. Slide parchment with bread onto large rimmed baking sheet. Cover with plastic wrap and let rise in warm draft-free area until very puffy, about 1½ hours.

Position rack in top third of oven and preheat to 350°F. Brush bread with egg glaze. Bake until golden, turning sheet after 15 minutes, about 25 minutes total. Slide parchment with bread onto rack and cool at least 1 hour. Serve warm or at room temperature. *(Can be made 1 day ahead. Cool completely, wrap in foil, and store at room temperature.)*

MAKES 1 LOAF

An interesting mix of brown sugar, pecans, and sea salt fills this woven lattice-top bread. You'll need a heavy-duty stand mixer with paddle attachment.

Whole Wheat Bran Muffins with Figs and Nuts

Nonstick vegetable oil spray

1 cup all purpose flour

½ cup whole wheat flour

½ cup oat bran

2 teaspoons ground cinnamon

2 teaspoons baking powder

1 teaspoon baking soda

½ teaspoon salt

1 cup (packed) diced dried Black Mission figs (about 6½ ounces)

½ cup chopped pecans

½ cup (packed) golden brown sugar

⅓ cup vegetable oil

2 large eggs

1¼ cups reduced-fat (2%) buttermilk

1 tablespoon vanilla extract

1 teaspoon grated lemon peel

Preheat oven to 400°F. Line 14 muffin cups with paper liners. Spray liners with nonstick spray. Whisk next 7 ingredients in bowl. Stir in figs and pecans. Whisk sugar and oil in large bowl. Whisk in eggs, then buttermilk, vanilla, and lemon peel. Mix in dry ingredients. Divide batter among cups.

Bake muffins until browned on top and tester inserted into center comes out clean, about 18 minutes. Cool on rack.

MAKES 14

Jalapeño and Honey Cornbread

1½ cups yellow cornmeal

¾ cup all purpose flour

3 tablespoons sugar

2 teaspoons baking powder

1½ teaspoons salt

1 teaspoon baking soda

1¼ cups buttermilk

2 large eggs

3 tablespoons butter, melted

3 tablespoons honey

2 tablespoons chopped drained canned pickled jalapeño chiles (en escabeche)

Preheat oven to 425°F. Butter 8-inch-diameter cake pan with 2-inch-high sides. Whisk first 6 ingredients in large bowl to blend. Whisk buttermilk, eggs, butter, honey, and jalapeños in medium bowl to blend. Add buttermilk mixture to dry ingredients, stirring just until combined.

Transfer batter to prepared pan. Bake cornbread until golden and tester inserted into center comes out clean, about 30 minutes. Let cool 10 minutes. Cut around pan sides to loosen. Turn bread out onto rack; turn over onto plate. Cut into wedges; serve warm.

MAKES 1 LOAF

Glazed Raspberry Heart Scones

<table>
<tr><td>2</td><td>cups all purpose flour</td></tr>
<tr><td>⅓</td><td>cup sugar</td></tr>
<tr><td>2</td><td>teaspoons baking powder</td></tr>
<tr><td>½</td><td>teaspoon salt</td></tr>
<tr><td>5</td><td>tablespoons chilled unsalted butter, cut into ½-inch pieces</td></tr>
<tr><td>1</td><td>cup plus 3 tablespoons whipping cream</td></tr>
<tr><td>⅓</td><td>cup (about) raspberry jam (do not use seedless)</td></tr>
<tr><td>½</td><td>cup powdered sugar</td></tr>
<tr><td>¼</td><td>teaspoon rose water (optional)</td></tr>
</table>

Rose water lends a subtle floral flavor to the scones; it can be found at some supermarkets, specialty foods stores, and Middle Eastern markets.

Preheat oven to 400°F. Mix flour, sugar, baking powder, and salt in large bowl. Add butter; rub in with fingertips until mixture resembles fine meal. Gradually add 1 cup cream, mixing until dough comes together. Turn dough out onto sheet of foil; pat to ½-inch thickness. Using 3-inch heart-shaped or round cookie cutter, cut out scones. Gather scraps; pat to ½-inch thickness and cut out additional scones. Using floured knife, start at point of each heart and cut horizontally halfway through scones; fill with 1 generous teaspoon jam (jam will show at edges). Transfer to baking sheet. Bake scones until brown, about 18 minutes. Transfer to rack; cool scones until slightly warm.

Meanwhile, mix powdered sugar, remaining 3 tablespoons cream, and rose water (if using) in bowl to blend. Spread glaze over scones. Serve slightly warm or at room temperature.

MAKES ABOUT 12

Sage and Pancetta Biscuits with Fontina Cheese

        1   3-ounce package thinly sliced pancetta (Italian bacon), chopped

        2   cups all purpose flour
        2   tablespoons sugar
     3½   teaspoons baking powder
       ½   teaspoon salt
        6   tablespoons (¾ stick) chilled unsalted butter, cut into ½-inch cubes
        1   cup coarsely grated Fontina cheese
        1   tablespoon chopped fresh sage
       ¾   cup plus 2 tablespoons chilled buttermilk

Preheat oven to 450°F. Sauté pancetta in medium nonstick skillet over medium heat until crisp, about 8 minutes. Remove from heat and cool.

Whisk flour, sugar, baking powder, and salt in large bowl to blend. Rub in butter with fingertips until coarse meal forms. Stir in Fontina and sage, separating strands of cheese. Add ¾ cup buttermilk and pancetta with any pan drippings and stir until moist clumps form. Turn dough out onto floured surface and knead just until dough holds together, about 4 to 6 turns. Flatten dough to ¾-inch thickness. Using 2¼-inch-diameter biscuit or cookie cutter, cut out rounds. Re-roll dough and cut out more rounds until all dough is used.

Transfer biscuits to large rimmed ungreased baking sheet, spacing apart. Brush biscuit tops with remaining 2 tablespoons buttermilk. Bake until biscuits are puffed and golden, about 14 minutes. Serve warm.

MAKES ABOUT 12

Soda Bread with Dark Chocolate and Candied Orange Peel

        3   cups unbleached all purpose flour
       ½   cup plus 2 tablespoons sugar
        2   teaspoons salt
        2   teaspoons baking powder
       ½   teaspoon baking soda
        6   tablespoons (¾ stick) chilled unsalted butter, cut into ½-inch cubes
        6   ounces bittersweet (not unsweetened) or semisweet chocolate, cut into ⅓-inch pieces
        6   ounces candied orange peel,* diced
     1¼   cups buttermilk
        1   large egg

Position rack in center of oven and preheat to 350°F. Line rimmed baking sheet with parchment paper; butter parchment. Whisk first 5 ingredients in large bowl to blend. Add butter; rub in with fingertips until mixture resembles coarse meal. Stir in chocolate and orange peel. Whisk buttermilk and egg in medium bowl to blend; add to dry ingredients. Stir just until incorporated.

Turn dough out onto floured work surface and knead gently just until dough comes together, about 5 turns. Form dough into 6½-inch-diameter round, about 2 to 2½ inches high. Transfer to prepared baking sheet. Using sharp knife, cut 1-inch-deep, 3-inch-long slits in top of bread, forming sunburst pattern.

Bake bread until well browned and very firm when pressed and tester inserted into center comes out clean, turning baking sheet halfway through baking, about 1 hour 10 minutes total.

Available in the produce section of most supermarkets.

MAKES 1 LARGE ROUND LOAF

Cutting notches in a sunburst pattern allows steam to escape while the bread is baking—and results in a crusty top with a nice design.

Lemon-Ginger Muffins

1 lemon
⅔ cup ½-inch cubes peeled fresh ginger
1 cup sugar, divided

2⅔ cups all purpose flour
1 teaspoon baking soda
½ teaspoon salt
1 cup buttermilk
2 large eggs
¼ cup vegetable oil
¼ cup (½ stick) unsalted butter, melted

Preheat oven to 350°F. Line 16 muffin cups with paper liners. Using vegetable peeler, remove peel (yellow part only) from lemon. Coarsely chop peel. Place peel, ginger, and ¼ cup sugar in processor. Process until moist paste forms.

Whisk remaining ¾ cup sugar, flour, baking soda, and salt in large bowl. Whisk buttermilk, eggs, oil, melted butter, and ginger mixture in medium bowl to blend well. Stir into flour mixture just to blend. Divide batter among prepared muffin cups. Bake until toothpick inserted into center comes out clean, about 25 minutes. Serve warm or at room temperature. (*Can be made 8 hours ahead. Cool completely and store in airtight container.*)

MAKES 16

Irish Soda Bread with Raisins

Nonstick vegetable oil spray
2 cups all purpose flour
5 tablespoons sugar, divided
1½ teaspoons baking powder
1 teaspoon salt
¾ teaspoon baking soda
3 tablespoons butter, chilled, cut into cubes
1 cup buttermilk
⅔ cup raisins

1 tablespoon melted butter

Preheat oven to 375°F. Spray 8-inch-diameter cake pan with nonstick spray. Combine all purpose flour, 4 tablespoons sugar, baking powder, salt, and baking soda in large bowl; whisk to blend. Add chilled butter. Using fingertips, rub in until coarse meal forms. Make well in center of flour mixture. Add buttermilk. Gradually stir dry ingredients into milk to blend. Mix in raisins.

Using floured hands, shape dough into ball. Transfer to prepared pan and flatten slightly (dough will not come to edges of pan). Brush dough with 1 tablespoon melted butter. Sprinkle dough with remaining 1 tablespoon sugar.

Bake bread until brown and tester inserted into center comes out clean, about 40 minutes. Cool bread in pan 10 minutes. Transfer to rack. Serve warm or at room temperature.

MAKES 1 LOAF

Dried-Cherry Scones

Nonstick vegetable oil spray
1¼ cups all purpose flour
3 tablespoons sugar
1½ teaspoons baking powder
¼ teaspoon salt
6 tablespoons (¾ stick) chilled unsalted butter, cut into ½-inch cubes
½ cup chopped dried tart cherries
⅓ cup buttermilk
1 large egg
2 teaspoons vanilla extract
1 teaspoon grated orange peel

Preheat oven to 400°F. Spray baking sheet with nonstick spray. Mix flour, sugar, baking powder, and salt in large bowl to blend. Add butter; rub in with fingertips until pea-size pieces form. Stir in cherries. Whisk buttermilk, egg, vanilla, and orange peel in small bowl. Add egg mixture to flour mixture; stir just until dough forms.

Shape dough into 6-inch round on prepared sheet. Cut into 8 wedges, spacing 1½ inches apart. Bake until golden, 15 minutes.

MAKES 8

Buffet Brunch for 8

Citrus-Blossom Gin Fizz
(page 35)

Scrambled Eggs

Bacon

Lemon-Ginger Muffins
(opposite)

Irish Soda Bread with Raisins
(opposite)

Butter and Assorted Preserves

Fruit Salad

Far Breton
(page 200)

Orange Juice

Coffee and *Tea*

Pear and Almond Tart
(page 178)

Desserts

Cream Cheese Crostata with Orange Marmalade

CRUST

1½ cups cake flour

4½ tablespoons sugar

½ large egg yolk

9 tablespoons (1 stick plus 1 tablespoon) chilled unsalted butter, cut into ½-inch cubes

Nonstick vegetable oil spray

FILLING

1 8-ounce package cream cheese, room temperature

¾ cup mascarpone cheese*

½ cup plus 1 tablespoon sugar

⅔ cup orange marmalade

½ cup sliced almonds, toasted

FOR CRUST: Mix flour and sugar together on work surface. Make well in center of mixture; add egg yolk. Scatter butter cubes over flour mixture. Using hands, gently mix ingredients together until well blended and dough forms. Flatten dough into disk; wrap in plastic and chill at least 1 hour or overnight.

Preheat oven to 400°F. Spray 9-inch-diameter tart pan with removable bottom with nonstick spray. Press dough onto bottom and up sides of prepared pan. Bake until golden

brown and cooked through, pressing with back of fork if crust bubbles, about 18 minutes. Cool crust in pan on rack.

FOR FILLING: Beat cream cheese, mascarpone cheese, and sugar in medium bowl until smooth. Spread filling evenly in cooled crust; chill 1 hour. Spread marmalade evenly over filling. Sprinkle almonds over. *(Can be made 1 day ahead. Cover; chill.)*

*Italian cream cheese; available at many supermarkets and Italian markets.

6 TO 8 SERVINGS

White Nectarine Galettes

2 cups all purpose flour
1 teaspoon plus 2 tablespoons sugar
½ teaspoon coarse kosher salt
¾ cup (1½ sticks) chilled unsalted butter, cut into ½-inch cubes
7 tablespoons (or more) ice water

6 white nectarines (about 2½ pounds), halved, pitted, thinly sliced
2 tablespoons fresh lemon juice
3 tablespoons unsalted butter, melted
2 tablespoons raw sugar*

A quick homemade pastry makes these free-form tartlets especially good. Keep the recipe handy and use with all sorts of fruit.

Blend all purpose flour, 1 teaspoon sugar, and salt in processor. Cut in unsalted butter, using on/off turns, until mixture resembles coarse meal. Add 7 tablespoons ice water; process until moist clumps form, adding more ice water by teaspoonfuls if dry. Gather dough into ball; flatten into disk. Wrap in plastic; chill 30 minutes.

Line 2 baking sheets with parchment paper. Cut dough into 8 pieces; roll into balls. Roll out each ball on floured surface to 6½-inch round. Transfer to prepared baking sheets. Chill 30 minutes.

Position racks in top and bottom thirds of oven; preheat to 400°F. Toss nectarines, lemon juice, and 2 tablespoons sugar in bowl. Divide fruit among crusts, leaving 1½-inch border. Fold border over fruit, pleating edges and exposing fruit in center. Brush crust edges with butter; sprinkle with raw sugar.

Bake galettes until fruit bubbles, reversing sheets halfway through baking, about 35 minutes. Cool galettes on rack 15 minutes. Serve warm or at room temperature.

*Also called turbinado or demerara sugar; available at most supermarkets and natural foods stores.

MAKES 8

Sour-Cherry Streusel Pie

1 Tender Pie Crust dough disk (see recipe)

STREUSEL

1¼ cups all purpose flour

6 tablespoons (packed) golden brown sugar

¼ cup sugar

¾ teaspoon ground cinnamon

¼ teaspoon salt

½ cup (1 stick) unsalted butter, melted

¼ teaspoon vanilla extract

FILLING

1 cup (scant) sugar

3½ tablespoons all purpose flour

1 teaspoon ground cinnamon

Pinch of salt

2½ pounds sour cherries, pitted

Roll out pie crust disk on floured surface to 13½-inch round. Transfer to 9-inch glass pie dish. Trim overhang to 1 inch. Fold edges under. Crimp, forming high rim (about ¼ inch above sides of dish). Chill at least 30 minutes and up to 1 day.

FOR STREUSEL: Mix first 5 ingredients in bowl. Add melted butter and vanilla; rub in with fingertips until small clumps form. (*Can be made 4 hours ahead. Cover; let stand at room temperature.*)

FOR FILLING: Position rack in center of oven; preheat to 375°F. Place foil-lined baking sheet in bottom of oven to catch spills. Mix first 4 ingredients in large bowl. Add cherries; toss to coat. Let stand until cherries begin to release juice, stirring occasionally, about 10 minutes. Transfer filling to chilled crust, mounding in center. Sprinkle streusel over, covering completely and pressing to adhere.

Bake pie 20 minutes. Tent loosely with foil. Bake until filling bubbles thickly and streusel is golden, about 1 hour 10 minutes longer. Cool on rack.

8 SERVINGS

Look for fresh sour cherries at farmers' markets. Or use Bing cherries instead and add 1 tablespoon fresh lemon juice to the filling.

Tender Pie Crust

    3   cups all purpose flour
    2   tablespoons sugar
 1¾   teaspoons salt
    1   cup plus 2 tablespoons (2¼ sticks) chilled unsalted butter, cut into
           ½-inch cubes
    8   tablespoons (or more) ice water
 1½   teaspoons apple cider vinegar

Blend flour, sugar, and salt in processor. Add butter; using on/off turns, process until coarse meal forms. Add 8 tablespoons ice water and cider vinegar; blend until moist clumps form, adding more ice water by teaspoonfuls if dough is dry. Gather dough together. Turn dough out onto work surface; divide dough in half. Form each half into ball and flatten into disk. Wrap disks separately in plastic; chill at least 1 hour. (*Can be made ahead. Keep dough chilled up to 2 days, or enclose in resealable plastic bag and freeze up to 1 month, then thaw in refrigerator overnight. Soften slightly at room temperature before rolling out.*)

MAKES 2 DOUGH DISKS (ENOUGH FOR TWO 9-INCH PIE CRUSTS)

Based on a classic pâte brisée, the buttery French pastry dough used for making pies and tarts, this pie crust dough is easy to work with and wonderfully versatile.

Peach Lattice Pie

2 Tender Pie Crust dough disks (see recipe on page 175)
1 egg white, beaten to blend

FILLING
1 cup sugar, divided
½ teaspoon (scant) ground cinnamon
Pinch of salt
3½ pounds firm but ripe peaches, peeled, halved, pitted, each half cut into 3 wedges
1 tablespoon fresh lemon juice

¼ cup water
2 tablespoons (¼ stick) unsalted butter
2 tablespoons whipping cream

3 tablespoons all purpose flour

1 egg yolk, beaten to blend with 2 teaspoons water (glaze)
1 tablespoon sugar mixed with ¼ teaspoon ground cinnamon (cinnamon sugar)

Position rack in center of oven and preheat to 375°F. Place foil-lined baking sheet in bottom of oven to catch any spills. Roll out 1 pie crust disk on lightly floured surface to 13½-inch round. Transfer to 9-inch-diameter glass pie dish. Trim overhang to 1 inch. Fold edges under and crimp decoratively, forming high rim (about ¼ inch above sides of dish). Chill crust 30 minutes. Line crust with foil; fill with dried beans. Bake crust until sides are set and pale golden, about 35 minutes. Transfer to rack; remove foil and beans. Brush warm crust with egg white. Cool completely.

Meanwhile, line another baking sheet with parchment paper. Roll out second pie crust disk on floured surface to 13½-inch round. Cut into ¾-inch-wide strips. Place strips on prepared baking sheet. Chill while preparing filling.

FOR FILLING: Combine ¼ cup sugar, cinnamon, and salt in large bowl. Add peaches and lemon juice and toss gently to coat. Let stand 30 minutes.

Meanwhile, stir remaining ¼ cup sugar and ¼ cup water in medium saucepan over medium heat until sugar dissolves. Increase heat; boil without stirring until syrup is deep amber, occasionally swirling pan and brushing down sides with wet pastry brush, about 11 minutes. Remove from heat. Add butter and cream (mixture will bubble vigorously); stir caramel until smooth. Strain juices from peaches into caramel; cool to lukewarm.

Preheat oven to 375°F. Add caramel and flour to peaches in bowl; toss gently. Transfer filling to crust, mounding in center.

Arrange 6 dough strips in 1 direction across top of pie, spacing apart. Working with 1 strip at a time, arrange 6 more strips in opposite direction atop first, lifting strips and weaving over and under, forming lattice. Gently press ends of strips to edge of baked bottom

crust to adhere. Trim overhang. Brush lattice strips (but not crust edge) with egg yolk glaze. Sprinkle strips with cinnamon sugar.

Bake pie 35 minutes. Tent pie loosely with foil to prevent over-browning. Continue to bake pie until filling bubbles thickly and lattice is golden brown, about 25 minutes longer. Cool pie on rack.

8 SERVINGS

The fruit is tossed with a peach caramel sauce (juices from the peaches combined with homemade caramel) that adds depth of flavor to the filling. Keep an eye on this pie as it bakes; it browns quickly and so needs to be tented with foil.

Pear and Almond Tart

PEARS

 4 cups water

1¼ cups sugar

1½ tablespoons fresh lemon juice

 3 medium-size firm but ripe Bosc pears, peeled (each about 7 ounces)

CRUST

½ cup powdered sugar

¼ cup blanched slivered almonds

¼ teaspoon salt

 9 tablespoons (1 stick plus 1 tablespoon) unsalted butter, room temperature

 1 large egg yolk

1¼ cups all purpose flour

ALMOND FILLING

⅔ cup blanched slivered almonds

 1 tablespoon all purpose flour

 7 tablespoons sugar

 6 tablespoons (¾ stick) unsalted butter, room temperature

 1 large egg

 Powdered sugar (optional)

FOR PEARS: Bring 4 cups water, sugar, and lemon juice to boil in large saucepan over medium-high heat, stirring until sugar dissolves. Add pears. Reduce heat to medium and simmer until pears are very tender, turning occasionally, about 20 minutes. Cool pears in syrup. *(Can be made 2 days ahead. Cover and refrigerate.)*

FOR CRUST: Blend powdered sugar, almonds, and salt in processor until nuts are finely ground. Add butter and blend until smooth, scraping down sides of bowl occasionally. Mix in egg yolk. Add flour. Using on/off turns, blend until dough comes together in clumps. Gather dough into ball; flatten into disk. Wrap in plastic and chill at least 3 hours. *(Can be made 2 days ahead. Keep refrigerated.)*

FOR ALMOND FILLING: Finely grind almonds and flour in processor. Mix in 7 tablespoons sugar, then butter, blending until smooth. Mix in egg. Transfer filling to medium bowl. Cover and chill at least 3 hours. *(Can be made 2 days ahead. Keep chilled.)*

Position rack in center of oven and preheat to 375°F. Roll out chilled dough on floured sheet of parchment paper to 12-inch round, lifting and turning dough occasionally to free from paper. Using paper as aid, turn dough into 9-inch-diameter tart pan with removable bottom; peel off paper. Seal any cracks in dough. Trim overhang to ¼ inch. Fold overhang in, making double-thick sides. Pierce crust all over with fork. Freeze crust 10 minutes.

Line crust with buttered foil, buttered side down, then fill with dried beans or pie weights. Bake crust until sides are set, about 20 minutes. Remove foil and beans. Bake crust until sides are golden and bottom is set, pressing with back of fork if crust bubbles, about 10 minutes longer. Cool crust in pan on rack. Reduce oven temperature to 350°F.

Spread almond filling evenly in crust. Stem pears and cut each in half lengthwise; scoop out cores. Cut each half crosswise into thin slices. Gently press each pear half to fan slices but keep slices tightly overlapped. Slide spatula under pears and arrange atop filling like spokes of wheel with narrow ends in center.

Bake tart until golden and tester inserted into center of filling comes out clean, about 55 minutes. Cool tart in pan on rack. Push pan bottom up, releasing tart from pan. *(Can be made 8 hours ahead. Let stand at room temperature.)* Cut tart into wedges; sprinkle with powdered sugar, if desired, and serve.

8 SERVINGS

If you want to save time, use canned pear halves. Just drain the canned pears, dry them very well, and carry on. To grind almonds for the tart crust, pulse them in the food processor with sugar and salt in ten-second intervals until finely ground.

Scottish Apple Pie

  2 refrigerated pie crusts (one 15-ounce package), room temperature
1½ pounds Granny Smith apples, peeled, cored, cut into ⅓-inch cubes
  9 tablespoons sugar, divided
  ½ cup gingersnap cookie crumbs
  ⅓ cup orange marmalade
  ⅓ cup golden raisins
  1 teaspoon grated orange peel

  1 tablespoon whipping cream

Crushed gingersnap cookies, orange marmalade, and raisins set this pie apart from the American version.

Preheat oven to 375°F. Line 9-inch-diameter glass pie dish with 1 pie crust. Mix apples, 8 tablespoons sugar, cookie crumbs, marmalade, raisins, and orange peel in large bowl. Spoon filling into crust-lined dish. Top with remaining crust. Press crust edges together to seal; crimp edge decoratively. Cut 1-inch hole in center.

Blend cream and 1 tablespoon sugar in small bowl; brush over crust. Bake pie until crust is golden and filling bubbles thickly, about 45 minutes. Serve warm.

8 SERVINGS

Lemon Meringue Blueberry Pie

LEMON CURD AND MOUSSE

1½ cups sugar

2¼ teaspoons cornstarch

¾ cup fresh lemon juice

9 large egg yolks

¾ cup (1½ sticks) unsalted butter, cut into ½-inch cubes

½ cup chilled heavy whipping cream

BLUEBERRY COMPOTE

1½ cups fresh blueberries (from two ½-pint containers), divided

3 tablespoons sugar

½ teaspoon fresh lemon juice

¼ teaspoon finely grated lemon peel

Pinch of salt

Pinch of ground cinnamon

1 teaspoon all purpose flour

CRUST

1 Tender Pie Crust dough disk (see recipe on page 175)

MERINGUE

3 large egg whites

½ cup sugar

FOR LEMON CURD AND MOUSSE: Whisk sugar and cornstarch in heavy medium saucepan to blend. Gradually add lemon juice, whisking until cornstarch dissolves. Whisk in yolks. Add butter. Cook over medium heat until curd thickens and boils, whisking constantly, about 8 minutes. Transfer curd to medium bowl. Press plastic wrap directly onto surface of curd. Refrigerate at least 1 day. *(Can be prepared 5 days ahead. Keep chilled.)*

Using electric mixer, beat whipping cream in medium bowl until peaks form. Fold ¾ cup lemon curd into whipped cream ¼ cup at a time. Chill lemon mousse at least 2 hours and up to 6 hours. Keep remaining curd chilled.

FOR BLUEBERRY COMPOTE: Combine ¾ cup blueberries, sugar, lemon juice, grated lemon peel, salt, and cinnamon in small saucepan. Stir over medium heat until sugar dissolves, about 4 minutes. Whisk in flour; cook 1 minute. Remove from heat. Stir in remaining ¾ cup blueberries. Transfer compote to small bowl. Cover and refrigerate at least 2 hours. *(Can be prepared 1 day ahead. Keep compote refrigerated.)*

FOR CRUST: Position rack in center of oven and preheat to 375°F. Roll out pie crust disk on lightly floured surface to 13½-inch round. Transfer crust to 9-inch-diameter glass pie dish. Trim overhang to 1 inch. Fold edges under and crimp decoratively; chill 30 minutes. Line crust with foil; fill with dried beans or pie weights. Bake crust until sides are set, about

20 minutes. Remove foil and beans from crust. Bake crust until golden and cooked through, piercing with fork if crust bubbles, about 20 minutes longer. Transfer crust to rack and cool completely.

Spread 1½ cups of remaining lemon curd over bottom of crust. Using slotted spoon and leaving most of juices behind, spoon ¾ cup blueberry compote evenly over curd. Drop lemon mousse in dollops over blueberries; spread to cover berries completely. Using slotted spoon, spoon remaining blueberries over mousse. Chill pie while preparing meringue.

FOR MERINGUE: Whisk egg whites and sugar in large metal bowl to blend. Place bowl over saucepan of simmering water (do not let bottom of bowl touch water); whisk constantly until sugar dissolves and mixture is very warm to touch, about 1½ minutes. Remove bowl from over water. Using electric mixer, beat mixture until thick and fluffy peaks form, about 5 minutes. Spoon meringue into pastry bag fitted with large (about ¾-inch) plain tip. Pipe meringue decoratively over top of pie, leaving 1-inch plain border to expose some of mousse and blueberries. Using pastry torch, singe meringue until golden. (*Can be prepared 6 hours ahead. Cover with cake dome and refrigerate.*)

8 SERVINGS

Rhubarb Lattice Pie with Cardamom and Orange

CRUST

 2 cups all purpose flour

 2 tablespoons sugar

 ¾ teaspoon salt

 ¾ cup (1½ sticks) unsalted butter, cut into ½-inch cubes, frozen 15 minutes

 7 tablespoons (about) ice water

FILLING

 10 cups 1-inch pieces rhubarb (about 2½ pounds)

 ⅔ cup plus 2 teaspoons sugar

 ¼ cup orange juice

 2½ teaspoons grated orange peel

 ½ teaspoon ground cardamom

 ¼ cup strawberry preserves

 1 tablespoon whipping cream

 Vanilla ice cream

FOR CRUST: Blend flour, sugar, and salt in processor 5 seconds. Add butter. Using on/off turns, blend until coarse meal forms. Add 6 tablespoons ice water. Using on/off turns, blend until moist clumps form, adding more ice water by ¼ tablespoonfuls if dough is dry. Gather dough into ball. Divide into 2 pieces, 1 slightly larger than the other. Flatten into disks. Wrap and chill at least 1 hour and up to 1 day.

FOR FILLING: Combine rhubarb, ⅔ cup sugar, orange juice, orange peel, and cardamom in large deep skillet. Toss over medium-high heat until liquid starts to bubble. Reduce heat to medium. Cover and simmer until rhubarb is almost tender, stirring very gently occasionally to keep rhubarb intact, about 8 minutes. Using slotted spoon, transfer rhubarb to colander set over bowl. Drain well. Add syrup from bowl to skillet. Boil until juices in skillet are thick and reduced to ⅔ cup, adding any additional drained syrup from bowl, about 7 minutes. Mix in preserves. Cool mixture in skillet 15 minutes. Very gently fold in rhubarb (do not overmix or rhubarb will fall apart).

Preheat oven to 375°F. Roll out larger dough disk on lightly floured surface to 12-inch round. Transfer to 9-inch glass pie dish. Roll out smaller dough disk to 11-inch round; cut into ¼-inch-wide strips. Spoon filling into pie dish. Arrange 6 dough strips atop filling, spacing evenly apart. Arrange 5 dough strips atop filling in opposite direction, forming lattice. Seal strip ends to crust edge. Stir cream and 2 teaspoons sugar in small bowl to blend. Brush over lattice, but not crust edge.

Bake pie until filling bubbles thickly and crust is golden, covering edge with foil if browning too quickly, about 55 minutes. Cool pie completely. Cut into wedges; serve with ice cream.

8 SERVINGS

Apple Crostata with Cinnamon-Almond Topping

CRUST

1 cup all purpose flour

½ teaspoon sugar

¼ teaspoon salt

6 tablespoons (¾ stick) chilled unsalted butter, diced

3 tablespoons (or more) ice water

CRUMB TOPPING

⅔ cup all purpose flour

6 tablespoons (packed) golden brown sugar

2 tablespoons yellow cornmeal

1¼ teaspoons ground cinnamon

⅛ teaspoon salt

6 tablespoons (¾ stick) chilled unsalted butter, diced

⅔ cup blanched slivered almonds

FILLING

7 tablespoons sugar, divided

1 vanilla bean, split lengthwise

4 large Pippin apples (2 to 2¼ pounds total), peeled, halved, sliced ¼ inch thick

3 tablespoons unsalted butter, melted, divided

FOR CRUST: Mix flour, sugar, and salt in medium bowl. Add butter. Cut in with back of fork until butter is reduced to oatmeal-size flakes. Add 3 tablespoons ice water. Toss until moist clumps form, adding more ice water by teaspoonfuls if dough is dry. Gather dough into ball; flatten into disk. Wrap and chill at least 1 hour and up to 1 day.

FOR TOPPING: Mix flour, brown sugar, cornmeal, cinnamon, and salt in bowl. Add butter. Blend with back of fork until moist clumps form. Mix in almonds.

FOR FILLING: Set rack at lowest position in oven; preheat to 400°F. Place 6 tablespoons sugar in large bowl. Scrape in seeds from vanilla bean; stir to blend well. Add apples. Add 2 tablespoons melted butter; toss to coat.

Roll out dough on floured sheet of parchment paper to 13½-inch round. Arrange apple filling in center, mounding slightly and leaving 2-inch plain border. Gently fold dough border over edge of filling, pleating loosely and pinching any cracks to seal. Brush dough border with remaining 1 tablespoon melted butter and sprinkle with remaining 1 tablespoon sugar. Sprinkle topping over exposed apple filling.

Slide rimless baking sheet under parchment and crostata and place in oven. Bake until crust is crisp and apples are tender, turning baking sheet after 20 minutes, about 40 minutes total. Run knife under crostata to loosen from paper. Cool on paper on baking sheet.

8 SERVINGS

Spiced Plum Pie

  2 Tender Pie Crust dough disks (see recipe on page 175)

  3 tablespoons plus 1 cup sugar
1¾ teaspoons ground cinnamon, divided
  2 tablespoons cornstarch
  2 teaspoons (packed) finely grated orange peel
  ¾ teaspoon ground cardamom
  ¼ teaspoon ground nutmeg
  ⅛ teaspoon ground cloves
  ¼ teaspoon salt
  ½ vanilla bean, split lengthwise
2½ pounds plums, halved, pitted, each half cut into 4 wedges

  2 tablespoons whipping cream

Roll out 1 pie crust disk on floured surface to 13½-inch round. Transfer to 9-inch glass pie dish. Trim overhang to 1 inch. Refrigerate crust while preparing filling.

Position rack in center of oven; preheat to 375°F. Place foil-lined baking sheet in bottom of oven to catch any spills. Mix 3 tablespoons sugar and ¼ teaspoon cinnamon in small bowl; set aside. Whisk 1 cup sugar, 1½ teaspoons cinnamon, and next 6 ingredients in large bowl. Scrape in seeds from vanilla bean. Add plums and toss to coat. Spoon filling into crust, mounding slightly in center.

Roll out second pie crust disk on floured surface to 13½-inch round. Drape crust over filling; trim overhang to 1 inch. Press top and bottom crust edges together Fold edges under; crimp. Using sharp knife, cut four 2-inch-long slits in center of top crust to allow steam to escape. Brush crust (but not edges) with cream. Sprinkle reserved cinnamon sugar over crust.

Bake pie 30 minutes. Tent pie loosely with foil to prevent overbrowning. Continue to bake until filling bubbles thickly through slits, about 1 hour longer. Cool completely on rack.

8 SERVINGS

Lemon Berry Shortcakes

3/4 cup sugar

2 tablespoons grated lemon peel

1/2 cup blueberry jam

2 tablespoons water

5 tablespoons lemon juice, divided

5 cups quartered hulled strawberries

4 1/2 cups fresh blueberries

2 1/3 cups chilled whipping cream, divided

2 cups all purpose flour

2 teaspoons baking powder

1/2 teaspoon salt

1/2 teaspoon ground nutmeg

Position rack in top third of oven; preheat to 400°F. Mix sugar and peel in small bowl. Melt jam in large skillet with 2 tablespoons water. Mix in 3 tablespoons lemon sugar, 2 tablespoons lemon juice, then berries. Set aside.

Combine 1 cup whipping cream, 2 tablespoons lemon sugar, and 1 tablespoon lemon juice in medium bowl and whip. Cover; chill.

Mix flour, baking powder, salt, nutmeg, and 1/3 cup lemon sugar in large bowl. Quickly mix in remaining 1 1/3 cups cream and 2 table-spoons lemon juice until dough just comes together. Drop dough by rounded 1/3 cupfuls in 6 mounds on ungreased baking sheet. Sprinkle dough with remaining lemon sugar. Bake biscuits until golden, about 23 minutes. Cool slightly on rack. Split biscuits; fill with mixed berries and whipped cream.

MAKES 6

Baked Apples Stuffed with Honey, Almonds, and Ginger

These are unusually light, with a crunchy filling. A dollop of thick, tangy Greek yogurt is a nice finishing touch.

- ¾ cup almonds, toasted, chopped
- ¼ cup (packed) golden brown sugar
- 2 tablespoons honey
- 1½ teaspoons finely grated lemon peel
- 1¼ teaspoons ground ginger
- ½ cup whipping cream

- 4 large (8- to 9-ounce) Fuji apples
- ¼ cup apple juice (preferably unfiltered fresh)

  Greek yogurt

Combine first 5 ingredients in small bowl. Mix in cream. Let stand until sugar dissolves and filling thickens, stirring occasionally, about 30 minutes.

Preheat oven to 350°F. Using small sharp knife and starting at side of apple at center point, cut around each apple to make slit in skin to prevent bursting. Using small end of melon baller, scoop out core and all seeds to within ½ inch of bottom. Place apples upright in 8x8x2-inch glass baking dish. Spoon filling into hollow of each apple. Mound remaining filling on top of each apple (some may slide down sides). Pour juice around apples. Butter large sheet of foil. Loosely tent dish with foil, buttered side down.

Bake apples until barely tender, about 1 hour. Uncover and bake until apples are very tender and sauce is bubbling thickly, about 20 minutes longer. Transfer apples and sauce to bowls. Serve with yogurt.

4 SERVINGS

Honey-Roasted Plums with Thyme and Crème Fraîche

½ cup (packed) dark brown sugar
¼ cup honey
4 tablespoons (½ stick) unsalted butter
½ cup fresh thyme sprigs
6 large assorted ripe but firm plums (about 2 pounds), halved, pitted

Crème fraîche
Additional fresh thyme sprigs

Preheat oven to 475°F. Stir first 4 ingredients in large ovenproof non-stick skillet over high heat until butter melts. Cook 2 minutes, stirring constantly (mixture will bubble vigorously). Add plum halves, cut side down. Cook plums without stirring for 2 minutes. Turn plums over and transfer skillet to oven. Roast until caramel is deep brown, checking frequently to prevent burning, about 4 minutes.

Divide plum halves among 6 plates. Spoon sauce from skillet over plums, leaving most of thyme sprigs behind. Drizzle plums with crème fraîche, garnish with additional thyme sprigs, and serve.

6 SERVINGS

For extra color, use different kinds of plums, such as bright red-fleshed Elephant Hearts, yellow Shiro plums, and pluots. (Avoid using Santa Rosas, which don't retain their shape when cooked.)

Berries in Sweet Fragolino Wine with Biscotti

2 ½ pint containers blackberries
2 ½-pint containers blueberries
2 ½-pint containers raspberries
3 cups halved stemmed small strawberries
½ cup sugar
3 cups (about 750 ml) chilled Fragolino or Moscato wine

Biscotti or other crisp cookies

Mix all berries in large bowl. Add sugar; toss to coat. Pour wine over. Cover and chill at least 30 minutes and up to 1 hour.

Divide berries and wine among 8 goblets. Serve with biscotti.

8 SERVINGS

Fragolino is a light dessert wine with fizz and the flavor of strawberries; use a Moscato if you can't find it.

Grilled Peaches and Apricots with Almond Crunch and Sweet Mascarpone

ALMOND CRUNCH
- 1 tablespoon unsalted butter
- 1 cup sliced almonds
- 2 tablespoons sugar
  Pinch of salt

FRUIT AND MASCARPONE

1	very large lemon
1	vanilla bean, split lengthwise
4	cups water
1½	cups sugar
1	1-inch-long piece fresh ginger, peeled, cut into thin rounds
¼	teaspoon cardamom seeds (from about 10 green cardamom pods)
3	large peaches, peeled, quartered, pitted
6	apricots, halved, pitted
1	8- to 9-ounce container mascarpone cheese*
2	tablespoons whipping cream
	Nonstick vegetable oil spray
	Mint sprigs

FOR ALMOND CRUNCH: Melt butter in large nonstick skillet over medium-low heat. Add almonds. Stir until nuts are golden, about 10 minutes. Sprinkle sugar and salt over. Stir until sugar melts and nuts glisten, about 3 minutes. Spread mixture out on piece of foil and cool. (*Can be made 2 days ahead. Store airtight at room temperature.*)

FOR FRUIT AND MASCARPONE: Using vegetable peeler, cut peel from lemon in strips; place in large saucepan. Squeeze ¼ cup lemon juice into saucepan. Scrape in seeds from vanilla bean; add bean. Add 4 cups water, sugar, ginger, and cardamom seeds. Bring to boil over high heat; stir until sugar dissolves. Reduce heat. Add peaches; poach 1 minute. Add apricots; poach 1 minute. Using strainer, transfer fruit to baking sheet; chill up to 6 hours. Boil syrup until reduced to 1 cup, about 15 minutes. Cool.

Blend mascarpone, cream, and 3 tablespoons reduced syrup in bowl. Cover and chill up to 4 hours.

Thread 2 peach quarters and 2 apricot halves onto each of 6 metal skewers. Arrange on platter.

Spray racks with nonstick spray; prepare barbecue (medium heat). Place pan with syrup on rack to rewarm. Grill fruit on skewers until slightly charred, basting with syrup, about 2 minutes per side. Transfer fruit to bowls. Sprinkle with almond crunch, drizzle with syrup, and spoon sweet mascarpone alongside. Garnish with mint.

Italian cream cheese; available at many supermarkets and Italian markets.

6 SERVINGS

Backyard Barbecue for 6

Speedy Gazpacho
(*page 24*)

Grilled Pork Chops with Chunky Andouille Barbecue Sauce
(*page 58*)

White Beans with Tomatoes and Spinach
(*page 140*)

Grilled Vegetables

Zinfandel

Grilled Peaches and Apricots with Almond Crunch and Sweet Mascarpone
(*opposite, pictured opposite*)

Banana Fritters with Coconut Ice Cream

½ cup rice flour*
⅓ cup all purpose flour
3 tablespoons sesame seeds
½ teaspoon salt
½ teaspoon baking powder
½ cup (about) cold water
4 large firm but ripe bananas, peeled, cut on slight diagonal into ½-inch-thick slices

Vegetable oil (for deep-frying)
Powdered sugar
Coconut or pineapple-coconut ice cream

Whisk first 5 ingredients in large bowl to blend. Whisk in ½ cup cold water. If needed, whisk in more water by tablespoonfuls until smooth thick batter forms. Add banana slices; gently stir to coat. (*Can be made 2 hours ahead. Let stand at room temperature.*)

Pour enough oil into heavy large saucepan to reach depth of 1½ inches. Attach deep-fry thermometer to side of pan and heat oil over medium-high heat to 350°F. Working in batches, add 3 or 4 coated banana slices to oil and cook until just golden brown, separating fritters if sticking together, about 4 minutes. Using slotted spoon, transfer fritters to paper towels. Sift powdered sugar over. Serve with ice cream.

Available at some supermarkets, specialty foods stores, and natural foods stores.

8 SERVINGS

Apricot-Raspberry Pavlovas with Sliced Almonds

4 large egg whites

1¾ cups plus 1 tablespoon sugar, divided

2 teaspoons cornstarch

¼ teaspoon almond extract

⅓ cup sliced almonds

1½ pounds apricots, halved, pitted, each half cut into 3 wedges

1 teaspoon vanilla extract

1 ½-pint container raspberries

1 cup chilled whipping cream

The components of these delicate meringue desserts can be made several hours ahead and assembled shortly before serving.

Preheat oven to 350°F. Line large rimmed baking sheet with parchment paper. Using electric mixer, beat egg whites in large bowl until soft peaks form. Gradually add 1 cup sugar; beat until thick and mixture resembles marshmallow creme, about 5 minutes. Beat in cornstarch and almond extract. Drop meringue onto prepared sheet in 6 mounds, spacing apart. Using spoon, make indentation in center of each. Sprinkle almonds over meringues. Place in oven; immediately reduce temperature to 250°F. Bake until meringues are dry outside but centers are still soft, about 45 minutes. Cool on sheet on rack 30 minutes.

Meanwhile, stir apricots and ¾ cup sugar in large nonstick skillet over medium-high heat until sugar dissolves and apricots are soft, about 5 minutes. Stir in vanilla. Transfer to bowl; chill until cool. Stir in raspberries.

Using electric mixer, beat cream with remaining 1 tablespoon sugar in medium bowl until peaks form.

Place meringues on plates. Spoon whipped cream into center of each. Top with apricot mixture and serve.

6 SERVINGS

The New-Wave Chocolate Birthday Cake

CAKE

- 4 ounces bittersweet or semisweet chocolate, chopped
- ⅓ cup (packed) dark brown sugar
- 2 tablespoons unsalted butter
- ½ teaspoon grated orange peel
- ½ teaspoon coarse kosher salt

- 2 large eggs
- 2 tablespoons sugar
- 1 tablespoon all purpose flour
- ½ cup hazelnuts, toasted, husked, chopped

FILLING

- 5 ounces bittersweet or semisweet chocolate, chopped
- 3 ounces high-quality milk chocolate (such as Lindt or Perugina), chopped
- 1½ cups chilled heavy whipping cream, divided

- 5 tablespoons unsalted butter, room temperature

GLAZE

- ½ cup heavy whipping cream
- 1 tablespoon light corn syrup
- 4 ounces bittersweet or semisweet chocolate, chopped
- 1 tablespoon unsalted butter, room temperature

  Large chocolate shards or curls (from 1- to 2-inch-thick 8-ounce piece bittersweet or semisweet chocolate)
  Additional toasted husked hazelnuts
  Candied orange peel strips*

FOR CAKE: Preheat oven to 325°F. Line 13x9x1-inch baking sheet with parchment paper; butter parchment. Combine first 4 ingredients in medium metal bowl. Set bowl over saucepan of barely simmering water; stir until chocolate and butter melt. Remove bowl from over water; stir in salt (mixture will be grainy).

Beat eggs and 2 tablespoons sugar in another medium bowl until pale, about 6 minutes; fold into chocolate mixture. Fold in flour, then hazelnuts. Spread batter evenly on baking sheet. Bake until tester inserted into center comes out with a few moist crumbs attached, about 13 minutes (cake will be thin). Transfer pan to rack. Cool cake completely.

FOR FILLING: Combine chocolates in medium metal bowl. Bring 1 cup cream to simmer in small saucepan; pour cream over chocolates and let stand 1 minute. Stir until melted and smooth. Chill mixture until firm, about 2 hours.

Place bowl with chilled chocolate mixture over saucepan of barely simmering water until mixture is partially melted (do not stir), about 5 minutes. Remove bowl from over water; add butter to bowl. Using electric mixer, beat until filling is thick and glossy, about

Birthday Party for 8

Crostini with Fresh Mozzarella
and Anchovy Sauce
(*page 18*)

Assorted Olives

Champagne

Roast Leg of Lamb with Mint,
Parsley, and Lima Bean Puree
(*page 54*)

Roasted Potatoes

Sautéed Spinach

Barolo

The New-Wave Chocolate
Birthday Cake
(*opposite, pictured at left*)

Vanilla Ice Cream

3 minutes. Using clean dry beaters, beat ¹/₂ cup chilled whipping cream in another medium bowl until peaks form. Fold into filling.

Cover 14x5-inch cardboard rectangle with foil. Invert cake onto work surface; remove parchment. Cut cake lengthwise in half. Place 1 cake half on foil-covered cardboard. Spread ¹/₂ cup chocolate filling over. Top with second cake half. Spoon remaining filling into pastry bag fitted with large plain round tip. Pipe filling atop cake in side-by-side lengthwise rows, then smooth top. Chill until filling is firm, about 1 hour.

FOR GLAZE: Bring cream and corn syrup to simmer in small saucepan. Remove from heat. Add chocolate; let stand 5 minutes. Stir until smooth. Add butter; stir until melted. Let stand until barely lukewarm but still pourable, about 20 minutes.

Place cardboard base with cake on rack set over rimmed baking sheet. Spoon glaze over top of cake, allowing glaze to run down sides. Using offset spatula, smooth glaze over sides. Mound chocolate shards or curls over top and sides of cake. Garnish with hazelnuts and candied orange peel. Refrigerate until glaze is set, at least 2 hours. (*Can be made 1 day ahead. Cover and keep chilled.*)

Available in the produce section of most supermarkets.

10 TO 12 SERVINGS

Toffee Crunch Caramel Cheesecake

GINGERSNAP CRUST

Nonstick vegetable oil spray

1½ cups ground gingersnap cookies (about 7¼ ounces)

5 tablespoons unsalted butter, melted

2 tablespoons (packed) golden brown sugar

CHEESECAKE

4 8-ounce packages cream cheese, room temperature

1 cup (packed) golden brown sugar

2 tablespoons (¼ stick) butter, melted

5 large eggs

1 teaspoon vanilla extract

CARAMEL TOPPING

1½ cups sugar

¼ cup water

½ teaspoon fresh lemon juice

1 cup heavy whipping cream

4 1.4-ounce English toffee candy bars (such as Heath or Skor), chopped

FOR GINGERSNAP CRUST: Preheat oven to 350°F. Spray bottom of 9-inch springform pan with 2½-inch-high sides with nonstick spray. Stir ground cookies, butter, and sugar in medium bowl until moist clumps form. Press firmly onto bottom of prepared pan. Wrap outside of pan with 3 layers of heavy-duty foil. Bake crust until firm and beginning to darken, about 14 minutes. Cool crust. Maintain oven temperature.

FOR CHEESECAKE: Beat cream cheese and sugar in large bowl until smooth. Beat in butter, then eggs, 1 at a time, until just blended. Beat in vanilla. Pour batter over crust in pan. Place springform pan in large roasting pan. Add enough hot water to come halfway up sides of springform pan. Bake cake uncovered until filling is puffed around edges and moves slightly in center when pan is gently shaken, about 1 hour 10 minutes. Remove pan from water; remove foil. Place hot cheesecake uncovered in refrigerator overnight.

FOR CARAMEL TOPPING: Stir sugar, water, and lemon juice in large saucepan over medium heat until sugar dissolves. Increase heat; boil without stirring until mixture turns deep amber, occasionally swirling pan and brushing down sides with wet pastry brush, about 9 minutes. Add cream (mixture will bubble). Reduce heat to medium-low. Simmer until reduced to 1¼ cups, stirring occasionally, about 8 minutes. Chill until thickened but still pourable, about 15 minutes.

Spoon caramel over top of cake just to edges (do not allow caramel to drip down sides). Garnish top edges with chopped English toffee. Chill at least 2 hours and up to 6 hours.

10 TO 12 SERVINGS

Yogurt Cake with Marmalade Glaze

1½ cups all purpose flour
2 teaspoons baking powder
¼ teaspoon salt
1 cup plain whole-milk yogurt
1 cup sugar
3 large eggs
1 teaspoon (packed) finely grated lemon peel
¼ teaspoon vanilla extract
½ cup vegetable oil

¼ cup lemon, orange, or grapefruit marmalade (for glaze)
1 teaspoon water

Position rack in center of oven and preheat to 350°F. Generously butter 8½x4½x2½-inch metal loaf pan. Sift flour, baking powder, and salt into medium bowl. Combine yogurt, sugar, eggs, lemon peel, and vanilla in large bowl; whisk until well blended. Gradually whisk in dry ingredients. Using rubber spatula, fold in oil. Transfer batter to prepared pan. Place pan on baking sheet.

Place pan on baking sheet in oven and bake until cake begins to pull away from sides of pan and tester inserted into center comes out clean, about 50 minutes. Cool cake in pan on rack 5 minutes. Cut around pan sides to loosen cake. Turn cake out onto rack. Turn cake upright on rack and cool completely. (*Can be made 1 day ahead. Wrap and store at room temperature.*)

Stir marmalade and 1 teaspoon water in small saucepan over medium heat until marmalade melts. Brush hot mixture over top of cake. Let glaze cool and set. Cut cake crosswise into slices.

8 SERVINGS

Meyer Lemon Buttermilk Pudding Cake with Fresh Berries

1½ cups buttermilk

1 cup sugar, divided

4 large egg yolks

⅓ cup fresh Meyer lemon juice

¼ cup all purpose flour

¼ cup (½ stick) unsalted butter, melted

⅛ teaspoon salt

3 large egg whites

Whipping cream
Assorted fresh berries

The Meyer lemon seduces pastry chefs with its fragrant perfume, mellow acidity, and sweetness. The fruit is thought to be a cross between a lemon and an orange or mandarin. Plant explorer Frank Meyer introduced the lemons from China into the United States in 1908. Look for them at specialty foods stores and farmers' markets from November through May.

Preheat oven to 350°F. Butter 8x8x2-inch glass baking dish. Blend buttermilk, ½ cup sugar, egg yolks, lemon juice, flour, butter, and salt in blender until smooth. Transfer buttermilk mixture to medium bowl. Using electric mixer, beat egg whites in large bowl until soft peaks form. Gradually add remaining ½ cup sugar and beat until stiff but not dry. Gently fold buttermilk mixture into whites in 3 additions (batter will be runny).

Pour batter into prepared dish. Place dish in roasting pan. Pour enough hot water into roasting pan to come halfway up sides of dish. Bake until entire top is evenly browned and cake moves very slightly in center but feels slightly springy to touch, about 45 minutes. Remove dish from roasting pan.

Cool cake completely in baking dish on rack. Refrigerate until cold, at least 3 hours and up to 6 hours. Spoon pudding cake out into shallow bowls. Pour cream around cake. Top with berries.

6 TO 8 SERVINGS

Far Breton

2 cups whole milk

3 large eggs

½ cup sugar

5 tablespoons unsalted butter, melted, cooled

¼ teaspoon vanilla extract

⅛ teaspoon salt

¾ cup all purpose flour

1 cup small or medium-size pitted prunes (about 6 ounces)

½ cup water

⅓ cup raisins

¼ cup Armagnac or other brandy

Powdered sugar

Combine milk, eggs, ½ cup sugar, butter, vanilla, and salt in blender jar. Blend 1 minute. Add flour and pulse just until blended, scraping down sides of jar. Cover and chill in jar at least 3 hours and up to 1 day.

Combine prunes, ½ cup water, and raisins in heavy small saucepan. Cook over medium heat until fruit is softened and water is almost evaporated, stirring occasionally, about 10 minutes. Turn off heat. Pour brandy over fruit. Using long match, ignite brandy. Let flames burn off, shaking pan occasionally. Transfer fruit to small bowl. Cool completely. *(Can be made 1 day ahead. Cover and let stand at room temperature.)*

Position rack in center of oven and preheat to 375°F. Butter 8-inch-diameter cake pan with

2-inch-high sides. Line bottom with parchment or waxed paper. Butter paper. Dust pan with flour, shaking out excess; place on baking sheet.

Reblend batter until smooth, about 5 seconds. Pour into prepared cake pan. Drop prunes and raisins into batter, distributing evenly. Bake cake on baking sheet until sides are puffed and brown and knife inserted into center comes out clean, about 1 hour. Cool cake completely in pan on rack.

Place piece of parchment or waxed paper on flat plate. Sift powdered sugar onto paper. Run knife around cake in pan to loosen. Invert pan onto paper, releasing cake. Remove pan and peel off paper. Place serving plate over cake and invert. Dust top of cake with additional powdered sugar.

8 SERVINGS

A *far breton* is a custardy pudding cake, similar to a *clafouti* but with a dense, smooth, flan-like texture. This one, studded with brandy-soaked prunes and raisins, is the signature pastry of Brittany. The batter is made in the blender. Go easy when you pulse in the flour. The idea is to just mix it into the batter, not to whip it so vigorously that you encourage the formation of gluten, which would toughen the finished cake.

Cornmeal and Fig Cake with Pine Nuts

    4 large egg yolks
   ⅔ cup sugar
    2 cups whole milk
   ¼ cup grappa
   ⅛ teaspoon salt
   ½ cup polenta (coarse cornmeal; do not use instant)

   ½ cup diced dried Calimyrna figs (about 6)
   ⅓ cup raisins
   ¼ cup pine nuts
    1 tablespoon fennel seeds

Polenta stands in for flour with delicious results in this Venetian dessert.

Preheat oven to 375°F. Butter 8-inch-diameter cake pan with 2-inch-high sides. Beat egg yolks and sugar in large bowl. Bring milk, grappa, and salt to boil in heavy medium saucepan over medium heat. Gradually whisk hot milk mixture into egg yolk mixture. Return to saucepan. Whisk in polenta. Whisk over medium-high heat until mixture thickens and begins to bubble, about 8 minutes.

Fold figs, raisins, pine nuts, and fennel seeds into polenta mixture. Pour into prepared cake pan.

Bake cake until golden brown, set in center, and beginning to pull away from sides of pan, about 40 minutes. Cool in pan 20 minutes. Cut around pan sides and invert cake onto platter. Serve warm or at room temperature.

6 SERVINGS

Chocolate-Peanut Butter Cake with Cream Cheese and Butterfinger Frosting

FILLING

2¼ cups heavy whipping cream
½ cup (packed) golden brown sugar
12 ounces bittersweet or semisweet chocolate, finely chopped
½ cup old-fashioned (natural) chunky peanut butter

CAKE

2½ cups all purpose flour
1 teaspoon baking powder
1 teaspoon baking soda
½ teaspoon salt
10 tablespoons (1¼ sticks) unsalted butter, room temperature
½ cup old-fashioned (natural) chunky peanut butter
1 pound golden brown sugar
4 large eggs
1 teaspoon vanilla extract
1 cup buttermilk

FROSTING

1½ 8-ounce packages cream cheese, room temperature
2 cups powdered sugar, divided
6 tablespoons (¾ stick) unsalted butter, room temperature
1 teaspoon vanilla extract

¾ cup chilled heavy whipping cream
   Butterfinger candy bars, coarsely chopped
   Glazed peanuts

FOR FILLING: Bring cream and sugar to simmer in saucepan, whisking to dissolve sugar. Remove from heat. Add chocolate; let stand 1 minute. Whisk until smooth. Whisk in peanut butter. Chill overnight.

FOR CAKE: Preheat oven to 350°F. Butter three 9-inch-diameter cake pans with 1½-inch-high sides. Line bottoms with parchment paper. Sift first 4 ingredients into medium bowl. Using electric mixer, beat butter and peanut butter in large bowl until blended. Beat in sugar. Beat in eggs, 1 at a time, then vanilla. At low speed, beat in flour mixture in 4 additions alternately with buttermilk in 3 additions.

Divide batter among pans and spread evenly. Bake cakes until tester inserted into center comes out clean, about 25 minutes. Cool cakes 5 minutes. Turn out onto racks; peel off parchment. Cool completely.

FOR FROSTING: Using electric mixer, beat cream cheese, 1¼ cups powdered sugar, butter, and vanilla in large bowl to blend. Whisk whipping cream and ¾ cup powdered sugar in

bowl until mixture holds medium-firm peaks. Fold into cream cheese mixture in 3 additions; chill until firm but spreadable, about 1 hour.

Place 1 cake layer, bottom side up, on 9-inch tart pan bottom. Spread with half of filling. Place another layer, bottom side up, on work surface. Spread with remaining filling; place atop first layer. Top with remaining cake layer, bottom side up.

Spread frosting over top and sides of cake. (*Can be made 1 day ahead. Cover with cake dome; chill. Let stand at room temperature 2 hours before continuing.*) Press candy and peanuts onto top of cake.

12 SERVINGS

Blueberry Hill Cupcakes

CUPCAKES

3¼   cups all purpose flour
1¼   cups sugar
  1   tablespoon baking powder
½   teaspoon coarse kosher salt
¼   teaspoon baking soda
  6   tablespoons (¾ stick) unsalted butter, melted
¼   cup canola oil
  2   large eggs
  1   cup buttermilk or low-fat yogurt
  1   cup whole milk
  1   teaspoon vanilla extract
  1   teaspoon grated lemon peel
1¼   cups fresh blueberries, frozen for 4 hours

FROSTING

2¼   cups powdered sugar
10   tablespoons (1¼ sticks) unsalted butter, room temperature
½   cup plus 2 tablespoons maple sugar*
½   teaspoon coarse kosher salt
1¼   teaspoons vanilla extract
  4   teaspoons (or more) whole milk

  1   cup chilled fresh blueberries
    Fresh mint sprigs (optional)

FOR CUPCAKES: Preheat oven to 350°F. Line two 12-cup muffin pans with paper liners. Sift flour and next 4 ingredients into large bowl. Whisk melted butter and oil in medium bowl. Add eggs; whisk to blend. Whisk in buttermilk, milk, vanilla extract, and peel. Add buttermilk mixture to dry ingredients; whisk just to blend. Stir in frozen blueberries. Divide batter among liners.

Bake cupcakes until tester inserted into center comes out clean, about 23 minutes. Transfer cupcakes to racks; cool.

FOR FROSTING: Combine first 5 ingredients in medium bowl. Add 4 teaspoons milk. Using electric mixer, beat until well blended and fluffy, adding more milk by teaspoonfuls if dry (small granules of maple sugar will still remain), about 4 minutes. Spread over cupcakes.

Garnish cupcakes with chilled berries, and mint sprigs, if desired. (*Can be made 4 hours ahead. Store in airtight container at room temperature.*)

Available at some supermarkets and natural foods stores.

MAKES 24

Dessert Buffet for 18

Champagne

Pear and Almond Tart
(page 178)

Chocolate-Peanut Butter Cake
with Cream Cheese and
Butterfinger Frosting
(page 202)

Blueberry Hill Cupcakes
(at left, pictured opposite)

Double-Lemon Bars
(page 232)

Apricot-Orange Shortbread Bars
(page 233)

Cheesecake

Chocolate Truffles

Strawberries

Coffee and *Tea*

Lemon Chiffon Layer Cake with Candied Rose Petals

CANDIED ROSE PETALS

2 large egg whites

½ cup sugar

Petals from 2 organic roses

CAKE

1 cup cake flour

14 tablespoons baker's sugar or superfine sugar, divided

1½ teaspoons baking powder

¼ teaspoon coarse kosher salt

3 large eggs, separated

6 tablespoons water

¼ cup canola oil

1 teaspoon grated lemon peel

¼ teaspoon whole cardamom seeds (removed from about 5 green cardamom pods)*

FROSTING

2½ cups chilled heavy whipping cream, divided

Pinch of saffron threads

⅔ cup powdered sugar

1 teaspoon rose water*

2 tablespoons natural unsalted pistachios

FOR CANDIED ROSE PETALS: Whisk egg whites in small bowl until foamy. Using pastry brush, brush rose petals on both sides with egg whites; sprinkle on both sides with sugar. Dry on nonstick rack at least 6 hours or overnight.

FOR CAKE: Preheat oven to 325°F. Butter two 8-inch-diameter cake pans with 1½-inch-high sides. Line pan bottoms with parchment paper; butter parchment. Sift flour, 7 tablespoons baker's sugar, baking powder, and salt into large bowl. Whisk yolks and next 4 ingredients in small bowl until smooth. Add yolk mixture to dry ingredients; whisk until smooth. Beat egg whites in medium bowl until soft peaks form. Gradually add 7 tablespoons baker's sugar; beat until whites resemble thick marshmallow fluff. Fold whites into batter in 3 additions.

Divide batter between prepared pans. Bake until cakes are golden and tester inserted into center comes out clean, about 25 minutes. Cool in pans on racks 15 minutes. Turn out onto racks, peel off parchment, and cool completely. (*Can be prepared 1 day ahead. Wrap and store at room temperature.*)

FOR FROSTING: Combine ½ cup cream and saffron in small saucepan. Bring to simmer. Remove from heat; let steep 20 minutes. Chill until cold.

Beat remaining 2 cups cream, powdered sugar, and rose water in large bowl until soft peaks form; strain in saffron cream. Beat until peaks form.

   Place 1 cake layer, flat side up, on platter. Spread 1 cup frosting over. Top with second cake layer, flat side down. Spread remaining frosting over top and sides of cake. Chill at least 1 hour and up to 6 hours. Garnish cake with rose petals and pistachios.

Rose water and cardamom pods are available at some supermarkets and at Indian and Middle Eastern markets.

8 SERVINGS

This chiffon cake filled with rose-scented whipped cream is inspired by the aromatics found in Persian, Turkish, and Indian confections. Cardamom seeds have more flavor than the ground powder and are like little explosions of spice in the cake.

Walnut Torte with Coffee Whipped Cream

    1   cup plus 6 tablespoons walnuts (about 5 ounces)

    4   large eggs, separated
    ½   cup sugar

    1   cup chilled heavy whipping cream
    3   tablespoons powdered sugar
    1   teaspoon instant coffee crystals dissolved in 2 teaspoons heavy
        whipping cream
    ¾   teaspoon vanilla extract
        Walnut halves

This flourless torte is made with a minimum of ingredients—nothing more than walnuts, eggs, and sugar—then generously coated with coffee-flavored whipped cream.

Preheat oven to 350°F. Using coarse grating disc (with large holes), grate walnuts in processor. Remove grating disc, leaving walnuts in processor bowl. Fit processor with metal blade. Using on/off turns, grind walnuts until finely ground but not pasty. Set aside 2 tablespoons ground walnuts for garnish.

Butter bottom (not sides) of 9-inch-diameter springform pan. Using electric mixer, beat egg yolks in large bowl until light and fluffy, about 4 minutes. Gradually add ½ cup sugar, beating until well blended. Stir remaining ground walnuts into yolk mixture. Using clean dry beaters, beat egg whites in another large bowl until stiff but not dry. Fold whites into nut mixture in 2 additions. Transfer to prepared pan.

Bake cake until tester inserted into center comes out clean, about 40 minutes. Cool 5 minutes. Run knife between cake and pan sides to loosen; remove pan sides. Cool cake completely on rack (cake will fall in center). (Can be prepared 1 day ahead. Cover and store at room temperature.)

Using electric mixer, beat cream, powdered sugar, coffee mixture, and vanilla in large bowl until peaks form. Spread coffee whipped cream onto top of cake. Sprinkle top with reserved ground walnuts; arrange walnut halves in center of cake. Cut cake into wedges.

8 SERVINGS

Chocolate-Brandy Bread Pudding with Cinnamon Whipped Cream

  1 tablespoon unsalted butter, melted
2¼ cups half and half
 ⅓ cup brandy
  3 cups (18 ounces) semisweet chocolate chips, divided
 ½ cup (packed) dark brown sugar
  1 teaspoon ground cinnamon, divided
  4 large eggs
  1 teaspoon vanilla extract
    Pinch of salt
  8 slices crustless country white bread (each about 5x4x½ inches), cut into ½-inch cubes
    (about 6 cups)

  2 cups chilled whipping cream
  2 tablespoons sugar

Brush 8x8x2-inch glass baking dish with 1 tablespoon melted butter. Simmer half and half and brandy in heavy large saucepan 3 minutes. Remove from heat. Add 1 cup chocolate chips. Let stand 1 minute, then whisk until chocolate is melted and mixture is smooth. Whisk in brown sugar and ½ teaspoon cinnamon. Let stand until cool, about 20 minutes. Whisk in eggs, then vanilla and salt. Stir in bread. Let stand 30 minutes.

Spread half of pudding mixture (about 2½ cups) in prepared dish. Sprinkle with 2 cups chocolate chips. Cover with remaining pudding mixture. *(Can be made 1 day ahead. Cover; chill.)*

Preheat oven to 350°F. Bake pudding uncovered until puffed and firm in center, about 45 minutes. Remove from oven; cool 10 minutes.

Beat chilled cream, sugar, and ½ teaspoon cinnamon in medium bowl until peaks form. Spoon pudding into bowls. Top with cream.

6 SERVINGS

Raspberries with Saba Sabayon

4   large egg yolks
¼   cup powdered sugar
4   tablespoons saba
2   tablespoons water
½   cup chilled whipping cream

12   ounces fresh raspberries

Whisk egg yolks, sugar, saba, and 2 tablespoons water to blend in top of double boiler over barely simmering water (do not allow upper pot to touch water); whisk constantly until mixture thickens and thermometer registers 160°F, about 4 minutes. Place top of double boiler over large bowl filled with ice; continue whisking until mixture cools, about 3 minutes. Whip cream in small bowl until soft peaks form; fold into saba mixture. Cover sabayon with plastic wrap and refrigerate until cold, at least 1 hour and up to 4 hours.

Divide berries among dessert coupes. Spoon sabayon over and serve.

4 SERVINGS

Saba (also known as *mosto cotto* or "cooked grape juice"), is a lightly sweet unfermented syrup made primarily from the must of Trebbiano grapes. When fermented and concentrated over years, *saba* becomes balsamic vinegar. It is available at specialty foods stores.

Marsala and Mascarpone Mousse with Pound Cake and Berries

½ cup sugar

⅓ cup plus 3 tablespoons imported sweet Marsala

3 egg yolks

1 cup (8 ounces) mascarpone cheese*

½ cup chilled whipping cream

½ teaspoon vanilla extract

¼ teaspoon cinnamon

24 4x½x¼-inch strips purchased pound cake

2 ½-pint containers raspberries

Whisk sugar, 1/3 cup Marsala, and yolks to blend in large metal bowl. Set over pan of barely simmering water (do not allow bowl to touch water); whisk constantly until mixture thickens and thermometer registers 160°F, about 6 minutes. Place bowl over large bowl filled with ice; continue whisking until custard cools, about 3 minutes.

Whisk mascarpone to loosen in another large bowl; in 3 additions, fold in custard. Whip cream, vanilla, and cinnamon in small bowl until soft peaks form; fold into custard.

Sprinkle pound cake strips with remaining 3 tablespoons Marsala. Arrange 4 strips in each of 6 goblets. Sprinkle a few raspberries over; top with 1/2 cup mousse. Sprinkle remaining raspberries over. Cover; chill 1 hour or overnight.

Italian cream cheese; available at many supermarkets and Italian markets.

6 SERVINGS

Coconut, Caramel, and Rum Flans

> 1 cup canned unsweetened coconut milk*
> 1 cup whipping cream
> 6 large egg yolks
> 1/2 cup sugar
> 1/4 cup purchased caramel ice cream topping
> 2 tablespoons dark rum
> 1 teaspoon vanilla extract
>   Pinch of salt
>
>   Toasted sweetened flaked coconut

Preheat oven to 350°F. Arrange six 3/4-cup custard cups or ramekins in 13x9x2-inch metal baking pan. Combine first 8 ingredients in medium bowl; whisk to blend. Pour custard into cups, dividing equally. Pour enough hot water into baking pan to come halfway up sides of custard cups.

Bake flans until set in center and golden brown on top, about 38 minutes. Remove flans from water. Chill uncovered until cold, about 3 hours. (*Can be made 1 day ahead. Cover and keep chilled.*)

Sprinkle flans with toasted coconut.

Available in the Asian foods section of most supermarkets.

MAKES 6

Dinner and a Movie for 6

Bruschetta

Rigatoni with Red Peppers, Wild Mushrooms, and Fontina
(page 126)

Tricolore Salad

Pinot Grigio

Marsala and Mascarpone Mousse with Pound Cake and Berries
(opposite, pictured opposite))

Espresso

Chocolate-Orange Pots de Crème with Candied Orange Peel

CANDIED ORANGE PEEL

- 1 orange
- 1 cup sugar, divided
- ¾ cup water

POTS DE CRÈME

- ⅔ cup whole milk
- ½ cup whipping cream
- 1 tablespoon Grand Marnier or other orange liqueur
- 1 teaspoon vanilla extract
- 1 teaspoon finely grated orange peel
- 4 ounces bittersweet (not unsweetened) or semisweet chocolate, chopped
- 4 large egg yolks
- 3 tablespoons sugar

  Lightly sweetened whipped cream

FOR CANDIED ORANGE PEEL: Using vegetable peeler, remove orange part of peel from orange in long strips. Cut peel lengthwise into ⅛-inch-wide strips. Stir ¾ cup sugar and ¾ cup water in heavy small saucepan over medium-low heat until sugar dissolves. Bring to boil. Reduce heat and simmer 2 minutes. Add orange peel; simmer 15 minutes.

Place remaining ¼ cup sugar in small bowl. Using slotted spoon, remove peel from syrup and transfer to sugar. Toss to coat. Cool, tossing occasionally. Cover bowl and let stand at room temperature overnight. (*Can be made 2 days ahead. Keep covered.*)

FOR POTS DE CRÈME: Preheat oven to 350°F. Bring milk, cream, Grand Marnier, vanilla, and grated orange peel to boil in heavy medium saucepan. Remove from heat. Add chocolate and stir until melted and smooth. Whisk yolks and sugar in medium bowl until pale yellow, about 2 minutes. Whisk egg mixture into chocolate mixture. Strain into 2-cup measuring cup.

Divide mixture between two 8-ounce custard cups. Place cups in small baking dish. Add enough water to baking dish to come halfway up sides of cups. Cover dish tightly with foil. Bake until custard is set, about 40 minutes. Remove cups from water in dish. Place in refrigerator uncovered until cool. Cover with plastic wrap and refrigerate until cold, about 6 hours. (*Can be made 2 days ahead. Keep refrigerated.*) Top with whipped cream, garnish with candied orange peel, and serve.

2 SERVINGS

Lemon Crème Brûlée with Fresh Berries

- 3 cups whipping cream
- 5 teaspoons grated lemon peel
- ¾ cup sugar
- 6 large egg yolks
- 2 teaspoons vanilla extract
- ¼ teaspoon salt

- 8 teaspoons golden brown sugar

- 2 ½-pint containers fresh raspberries
- ¼ cup Chambord (black-raspberry liqueur) or crème de cassis (black-currant liqueur)

Preheat oven to 325°F. Arrange eight ¾-cup custard cups or ramekins in 13x9x2-inch metal baking pan. Combine cream and lemon peel in heavy small saucepan and bring to simmer. Whisk sugar and yolks in large bowl until thick, about 3 minutes. Gradually whisk in hot cream mixture, then vanilla and salt. Let stand 10 minutes. Strain custard, then divide among cups. Pour enough hot water into baking pan to come halfway up sides of cups.

Bake custards until just set in center, about 55 minutes. Remove custards from water bath; chill uncovered until firm, at least 3 hours. (*Can be made 1 day ahead. Cover and keep refrigerated.*)

Preheat broiler. Place custard cups on baking sheet. Strain brown sugar through small sieve onto custards, dividing equally. Broil until sugar melts and browns, about 2 minutes. Chill until topping is hard and crisp, at least 1 hour and up to 2 hours.

Combine raspberries and liqueur in bowl. Let stand at room temperature at least 15 minutes and up to 1 hour. Spoon berry mixture atop custards and serve.

8 SERVINGS

Sweet-Cherry Clafouti

1 cup sugar, divided
½ cup chilled mascarpone cheese or crème fraîche
½ cup heavy whipping cream, divided
2 tablespoons kirsch (clear cherry brandy), divided

1 pound frozen pitted sweet cherries, thawed
3 large eggs
1 vanilla bean, split lengthwise
¾ cup sour cream
½ cup whole milk
6 tablespoons all purpose flour

A French country dessert that's like pudding and tender cake all in one.

Using electric mixer, beat 2 tablespoons sugar, mascarpone, ¼ cup whipping cream, and 1 tablespoon kirsch in medium bowl until peaks form. Cover and chill topping until ready to use.

Preheat oven to 375°F. Butter 10-inch glass pie dish; sprinkle with 1 tablespoon sugar to coat. Place cherries in single layer in dish. Place eggs and ¾ cup sugar in large bowl. Scrape in seeds from vanilla bean; discard bean. Whisk until blended and frothy. Whisk in ¾ cup sour cream, milk, remaining ¼ cup cream, and 1 tablespoon kirsch. Sift flour over and whisk to blend. Pour batter over cherries. Sprinkle with remaining 1 tablespoon sugar.

Bake clafouti until puffed, golden brown, and set in center, about 35 minutes. Serve clafouti directly from dish warm or at room temperature with mascarpone topping.

8 SERVINGS

Lemon and Amaretti Semifreddo with Raspberry Sauce

 2 10-ounce packages frozen raspberries in syrup, thawed

 4 large egg whites
 1 cup powdered sugar, divided
 2 cups chilled heavy whipping cream
 1 teaspoon finely grated lemon peel
⅛ teaspoon ground cinnamon
 1 cup coarsely crushed amaretti cookies (Italian macaroons; about 3 ounces), divided

Puree raspberries with syrup in blender. Strain puree into medium bowl; discard seeds. Cover; chill. (*Can be made 2 days ahead. Keep chilled.*)

Line 7- to 8-cup loaf pan or other mold with 2 layers of plastic wrap, leaving long overhang. Freeze pan. Using electric mixer, beat egg whites in medium bowl until soft peaks form. Add ¼ cup powdered sugar; beat until stiff but not dry. Using same beaters, beat cream and remaining ¾ cup powdered sugar in large bowl until peaks form. Fold in lemon peel and cinnamon. Fold large spoonful of cream mixture into whites, then fold whites back into cream in 2 additions. Fold in ¾ cup amaretti. Transfer mixture to prepared pan. Cover with plastic wrap overhang, then foil. Freeze at least 4 hours. (*Can be made 2 days ahead. Keep frozen.*)

Remove foil and open plastic. Turn semifreddo out onto platter. Remove pan; peel off plastic. Sprinkle with remaining ¼ cup amaretti. Serve semifreddo with sauce.

8 TO 10 SERVINGS

Fresh Strawberry Granita

    1 cup hot water
    ¾ cup sugar
    2 tablespoons fresh lemon juice
    3 cups sliced hulled strawberries (1 pound whole berries) plus
        additional berries for garnish

Stir first 3 ingredients in small bowl until sugar dissolves. Blend 3 cups strawberries in processor until smooth. Add sugar syrup and blend until combined.

Pour mixture into 13x9x2-inch nonstick metal baking pan. Freeze until icy around edges, about 25 minutes. Using fork, stir icy portions into middle of pan. Freeze until mixture is frozen, stirring edges into center every 20 to 30 minutes, about 1½ hours. Using fork, scrape granita into flaky crystals. Cover tightly and freeze. (*Can be made 1 day ahead. Keep frozen.*) Scrape granita into bowls. Garnish with berries.

MAKES ABOUT 6 CUPS

Mediterranean Dinner for 8

Carrot Soup with Orange and Tarragon
(*double recipe; page 30*)

Cedar-Planked Monkfish with Fire-Roasted Puttanesca Relish
(*double recipe; page 89*)

Couscous with Peas

Sautéed Zucchini

Riesling

Lemon and Amaretti Semifreddo with Raspberry Sauce
(*opposite, pictured opposite*)

Limoncello

Dulce de Leche Ice Cream Sundaes

CHOCOLATE SAUCE

1½ cups whipping cream
10 ounces bittersweet (not unsweetened) or semisweet chocolate, chopped

STREUSEL

½ cup all purpose flour
¼ cup sugar
3 tablespoons unsalted butter, room temperature
⅛ teaspoon salt

BLONDIES

6 tablespoons (¾ stick) unsalted butter, room temperature
½ cup sugar
¼ cup (packed) dark brown sugar
1 large egg
¼ teaspoon vanilla extract
¾ cup all purpose flour
¼ teaspoon baking soda
⅛ teaspoon salt
½ cup semisweet chocolate chips

2 pints dulce de leche ice cream
Whipped cream

FOR CHOCOLATE SAUCE: Bring cream to simmer in medium saucepan. Remove from heat. Add chocolate. Whisk until smooth.

FOR STREUSEL: Preheat oven to 350°F. Mix all ingredients in bowl. Rub together with fingertips until small clumps form. Spread on rimmed baking sheet. Bake until golden, stirring occasionally, about 18 minutes. Cool streusel on sheet.

FOR BLONDIES: Preheat oven to 350°F. Butter 8x8x2-inch metal baking pan. Using electric mixer, beat butter and both sugars in bowl to blend. Beat in egg, then vanilla. Sift flour, baking soda, and salt over; beat just until combined. Stir in chocolate chips. Spread batter in pan. Bake until golden around edges and tester inserted into center comes out clean, about 23 minutes. Cool in pan on rack.

Cut blondies into 1-inch squares. Arrange 5 squares in bottom of each dish. Rewarm chocolate sauce; spoon over. Top with ice cream, more sauce, then streusel and whipped cream.

MAKES 8

Southwestern Dinner for 8

Quesadillas

Margaritas

Beef Chili

Mixed Green Salad

Jalapeño and Honey Cornbread
(page 164)

Porter and *Ale*

Dulce de Leche
Ice Cream Sundaes
(at left, pictured opposite)

Mint-Truffle Ice Cream Terrine with Mint and Chocolate Sauces

---

TRUFFLES AND CHOCOLATE SAUCE

1½ cups heavy whipping cream

16 ounces bittersweet or semisweet chocolate, chopped

2 teaspoons pure peppermint extract

Unsweetened cocoa powder

5 cups (2½ pints) vanilla ice cream, slightly softened

MINT SAUCE

¾ cup sugar

⅓ cup water

2 cups (lightly packed) fresh mint leaves

FOR TRUFFLES AND CHOCOLATE SAUCE: Bring cream to simmer in heavy large saucepan; remove from heat. Add chocolate; let stand 1 minute. Whisk until mixture is smooth. Whisk in extract. Freeze until firm, about 4 hours, or chill overnight.

Line baking sheet with foil. Drop scant 1 tablespoon chocolate mixture for each of 16 truffles onto prepared sheet. Dust hands with cocoa; roll chocolate mounds into rounds. Cover and freeze truffles. Cover and chill remaining chocolate mixture for sauce. (*Truffles and sauce can be made 2 days ahead.*)

Line 8½x4½x2½-inch metal loaf pan with plastic wrap, leaving long overhang. Spread ⅓ of ice cream (about 1⅔ cups) over bottom of prepared pan. Press 8 truffles in random pattern (and spaced apart) into ice cream layer. Spread ½ of remaining ice cream over. Press remaining 8 truffles in random pattern (and spaced apart) into second ice cream layer. Spread remaining ice cream over. Cover terrine with plastic wrap overhang. Freeze at least 6 hours and up to 2 days.

FOR MINT SAUCE: Bring sugar and ⅓ cup water to boil in small saucepan, stirring until sugar dissolves. Pour syrup into blender; cool 10 minutes. Add mint to syrup and puree. Transfer sauce to bowl; cool. (*Can be made 1 day ahead. Cover and chill. Whisk to blend before using.*)

Stir chocolate sauce over low heat until warm. Transfer to pitcher. Turn ice cream terrine out onto platter; peel off plastic. Cut terrine into slices; arrange on plates. Drizzle chocolate sauce and mint sauce around terrine.

12 SERVINGS

Mint-chocolate truffles frozen in vanilla ice cream create a polka-dot dessert.

Sweet Cherry Sorbetto

½ cup hot water
½ cup sugar
½ cup orange juice
½ teaspoon vanilla extract
¼ teaspoon almond extract

1 16-ounce bag frozen pitted dark sweet
   cherries, thawed, juices reserved

Stir first 5 ingredients in bowl until sugar dissolves.

Blend cherries and reserved cherry juices in processor until cherries are coarsely chopped. Add sugar syrup; blend until smooth.

Process cherry mixture in ice cream maker. Transfer sorbetto to container; cover tightly and freeze until solid, at least 3 hours. (*Can be made 2 days ahead. Keep frozen.*)

MAKES ABOUT 3½ CUPS

Zabaglione Gelato

- 4 large egg yolks
- ½ cup sugar
- 1 cup whole milk
- 1 cup heavy whipping cream
- 6 tablespoons imported dry Marsala
- 2 tablespoons dark rum
- 1 teaspoon vanilla extract

Whisk yolks and sugar in medium bowl until thick, about 2 minutes. Heat milk and cream in medium saucepan over medium heat until mixture bubbles at edges. Gradually whisk hot milk mixture into yolk mixture; return to saucepan. Stir over medium heat until custard leaves path on back of spoon when finger is drawn across and temperature registers 170°F, about 6 minutes. Immediately pour custard through sieve set over another medium bowl. Stir Marsala, rum, and vanilla into custard. Cover; refrigerate at least 3 hours.

Process custard in ice cream maker. Transfer gelato to container. Cover and freeze until firm, at least 6 hours. *(Can be made 2 days ahead. Keep frozen.)*

MAKES ABOUT 3½ CUPS

Root Beer Granita Float

- 8 cups root beer
- 1 pint vanilla ice cream

Pour 4 cups root beer into 13x9x2-inch baking pan; freeze until set, 4 hours or overnight.

Meanwhile, boil remaining 4 cups root beer in large saucepan until reduced to ½ cup, about 30 minutes. Cool root beer syrup.

Using tines of fork, scrape frozen root beer into icy flakes, then mix gently in pan to blend. Spoon ¾ cup root beer granita into each of 6 clear glasses or dessert cups. Top granita with scoop of ice cream. Drizzle each with 4 teaspoons root beer syrup and serve.

6 SERVINGS

Chocolate-Cherry, Pistachio, and Raspberry Ice Cream Cake

½   cup dried tart cherries
½   cup orange juice

1   5.5-ounce package amaretti cookies*
¼   cup almonds, toasted
5   tablespoons unsalted butter, melted

1½   pints chocolate ice cream, softened
1   3-ounce bar imported milk chocolate, chopped
1½   pints raspberry sorbet, softened
1½   pints pistachio ice cream, softened
1   tablespoon grated orange peel

Chocolate curls or additional amaretti cookies
Hot Fudge Sauce (see recipe)

Boil dried tart cherries and orange juice in heavy small saucepan until all liquid is absorbed, stirring often, about 8 minutes. Remove pan from heat; cool completely.

Line 9x9x2-inch metal baking pan with foil, extending over sides of pan. Finely grind cookies and almonds in processor; add butter and process until moist crumbs form. Press crumbs onto bottom of foil-lined pan. Place in freezer.

Mix chocolate ice cream, chopped chocolate, and cherry mixture in medium bowl. Spoon over crust; smooth top. Freeze 30 minutes. Top with raspberry sorbet; smooth top. Freeze 30 minutes. Mix pistachio ice cream and orange peel in another medium bowl. Spoon over sorbet; smooth top (ice cream will come all the way up to top of pan). Cover and freeze until firm, at least 4 hours or overnight.

Using foil as aid, lift ice cream cake from pan; peel off foil. Use spatula dipped into hot water to smooth sides of cake. Transfer cake to platter. Garnish top of cake with chocolate curls or amaretti cookies dipped halfway into room-temperature Hot Fudge Sauce. Cut cake into squares. Serve with Hot Fudge Sauce.

Light, airy Italian almond macaroons that are available at some supermarkets and Italian markets.

8 SERVINGS

Inspired by Neapolitan ice cream, this pretty dessert layers cherry-studded chocolate ice cream with pistachio ice cream and raspberry sorbet. The press-in, no-bake crust is made with Italian amaretti cookies.

Hot Fudge Sauce

 1 cup whipping cream
½ cup light corn syrup
 6 ounces semisweet chocolate, chopped
 6 ounces bittersweet (not unsweetened) chocolate, chopped

Bring cream and corn syrup to simmer in heavy medium saucepan. Remove from heat. Add all chocolate and stir until melted and smooth. *(Can be made 2 days ahead. Cover and refrigerate. Rewarm Hot Fudge Sauce over medium-low heat just until heated through before serving.)*

MAKES ABOUT 2 CUPS

Grapefruit-Ginger Sherbet

 3 cups strained fresh ruby-red grapefruit juice, divided
¾ cup sugar
¼ cup grated peeled fresh ginger with juices
 1 tablespoon grated grapefruit peel

¼ cup light corn syrup
 1 cup buttermilk
½ cup whipping cream

Stir 1 cup grapefruit juice, sugar, ginger with juices, and grapefruit peel in heavy medium saucepan over medium-high heat until sugar dissolves. Bring to boil; remove from heat. Cool 30 minutes.

Whisk corn syrup, then buttermilk into ginger mixture. Stir in remaining 2 cups juice. Strain mixture into large bowl, pressing on solids to extract juices. Process in ice cream maker according to manufacturer's instructions. When sherbet is softly set, gradually pour in cream. Process 5 minutes longer to blend well. Transfer sherbet to container; cover and freeze.

MAKES ABOUT 4¼ CUPS

This sherbet is the perfect ending to an Asian-themed meal.

Desserts/Frozen Desserts **227**

Earl Grey Tea Madeleines with Honey

5 tablespoons unsalted butter plus additional for molds, room temperature
2 tablespoons loose tea leaves or tea from 2 tea bags (preferably Earl Grey)

¾ cup all purpose flour
½ teaspoon baking powder
   Pinch of salt
2 large eggs
⅓ cup sugar
2 tablespoons honey
2 teaspoons vanilla extract
½ teaspoon (packed) finely grated lemon peel

Line small sieve with 2 layers of damp cheesecloth and set sieve over small bowl. Melt 5 tablespoons butter in saucepan over low heat. Mix in tea. Let stand 10 minutes; pour into sieve. Twist cheesecloth tightly around tea mixture, releasing tea-flavored butter into bowl.

Sift flour, baking powder, and salt into medium bowl. Using electric mixer, beat eggs and sugar in large bowl until thick, about 4 minutes. Add honey, vanilla, and lemon peel; beat 1 minute longer. Gently fold in dry ingredients, then tea-flavored butter. Press plastic wrap onto surface of batter; chill batter at least 3 hours and up to 1 day.

Position rack in center of oven and preheat to 400°F. Brush twelve 3x2-inch madeleine molds with butter. Dust with flour; tap out excess. Place pan on baking sheet. Drop 1 scant tablespoon batter into each mold (batter will spread while baking, filling molds completely).

Bake madeleines until golden and tester inserted into center comes out clean, about 10 minutes. Sharply rap pan on work surface to loosen, then turn out onto rack. Serve warm or at room temperature.

MAKES 12

These little scallop-shaped cakes are a classic teatime treat in France.

Triple-Chocolate Cookies

10 ounces bittersweet (not unsweetened) or semisweet chocolate, chopped

½ cup plus 2 teaspoons all purpose flour
3 tablespoons unsweetened cocoa powder
¼ teaspoon baking powder
¼ teaspoon salt
1 cup plus 1 tablespoon sugar
5 tablespoons unsalted butter, room temperature
3 large eggs
1½ teaspoons vanilla extract
6 ounces (1 cup) semisweet chocolate chips

Position rack in center of oven and preheat to 350°F. Line 2 large rimmed baking sheets with parchment paper. Stir chopped chocolate in top of double boiler set over simmering water until melted and smooth; remove from over water. Cool melted chocolate 10 minutes.

Meanwhile, sift flour, cocoa powder, baking powder, and salt into medium bowl. Using electric mixer, beat sugar and butter in another medium bowl until crumbly. Add eggs, 1 at a time, beating well after each addition. Continue to beat until mixture is light, pale, and creamy, about 5 minutes. Add lukewarm melted chocolate and vanilla and beat just until blended. Fold in dry ingredients, then chocolate chips.

Drop chocolate cookie batter by ¼ cupfuls onto prepared baking sheets, spacing 2 inches apart. Bake cookies, 1 baking sheet at a time, until tops are evenly cracked but cookies are not yet firm to touch, about 16 minutes. Cool cookies completely on baking sheets.

MAKES ABOUT 16

Lemon-Walnut Biscotti

     3 cups all purpose flour
     1 teaspoon salt
     1 teaspoon baking powder
    ¼ teaspoon baking soda
    10 tablespoons (1¼ sticks) unsalted butter, room temperature
    1⅓ cups sugar
    1½ tablespoons finely grated lemon peel
     2 large eggs
     3 tablespoons fresh lemon juice
     3 cups chopped walnuts

     1 large egg, beaten to blend (for glaze)
        Raw sugar*

Whisk flour, salt, baking powder, and baking soda in medium bowl. Using electric mixer, beat butter, 1⅓ cups sugar, and lemon peel in large bowl until blended. Add 2 eggs, 1 at a time, beating just to blend after each addition. Beat in lemon juice, then flour mixture. Stir in walnuts.

Divide dough into 3 equal pieces. Place each piece on sheet of plastic wrap. Using plastic wrap as aid, form dough into 8-inch-long logs. Press logs slightly, flattening to 2½-inch-wide logs. Enclose in plastic wrap and chill until firm, at least 3 hours and up to 3 days.

Position rack in upper third of oven and preheat to 325°F. Line heavy large rimmed baking sheet with parchment paper. Unwrap logs, leaving on plastic. Brush top of logs with egg glaze. Sprinkle with raw sugar. Lift logs from plastic and transfer to prepared baking sheet, spacing evenly. Bake until golden brown and just firm to touch, about 50 minutes. Transfer to rack and cool completely. Reduce oven temperature to 300°F.

Line 2 heavy rimmed baking sheets with parchment paper. Using long serrated knife, carefully cut logs crosswise into ⅓-inch-thick slices. Arrange biscotti, cut side down, on prepared baking sheets. Bake cookies until golden brown around edges, about 20 minutes. Cool completely (biscotti will crisp as they cool). *(Can be made 3 days ahead. Store in airtight container at room temperature.)*

*Also called turbinado or demerara sugar; available at most supermarkets and natural foods stores.

MAKES ABOUT 5 DOZEN

Hazelnut Tozzetti

Nonstick vegetable oil spray
2½ cups all purpose flour
1½ cups sugar
 ¼ teaspoon baking powder
 ¼ teaspoon salt
  3 large eggs, beaten to blend
  2 cups whole hazelnuts, toasted, husked

These little biscotti are nutty and crunchy—and hard to resist. Serve them with coffee or tea, ice cream, or fruit. Better yet, dip them into a sweet dessert wine, like Italy's Vin Santo.

Preheat oven to 375°F. Spray large baking sheet with nonstick spray. Mix flour, sugar, baking powder, and salt in large bowl. Mix in eggs, then hazelnuts. Using moistened hands to keep dough from sticking, shape dough on prepared sheet into 16x3½x1½-inch log. Bake log until golden, about 25 minutes.

Reduce oven temperature to 325°F. Cool cookie log 30 minutes on sheet; carefully transfer to work surface. Using serrated knife, cut log crosswise and on slight diagonal into ⅓-inch-thick slices. Place slices, cut side down, on same baking sheet. Bake until golden, about 30 minutes. Cool tozzetti completely on sheet. (*Can be made 2 days ahead. Store airtight at room temperature.*)

MAKES ABOUT 30

Double-Lemon Bars

1 cup (2 sticks) unsalted butter, room
   temperature
⅔ cup powdered sugar
2¼ cups all purpose flour

2 cups sugar
4 large eggs
7 tablespoons fresh lemon juice with pulp
¼ cup finely grated lemon peel (from about 6
   large lemons)
1 teaspoon baking powder

Additional powdered sugar

Preheat oven to 350°F. Using electric mixer, beat butter in large bowl until fluffy. Beat in ⅔ cup powdered sugar. Add 2 cups all purpose flour, 1 cup at a time, beating until moist clumps form. Using back of fork, press dough over bottom of nonstick 13x9x2-inch metal baking pan. Bake crust until light golden, about 20 minutes.

Meanwhile, beat 2 cups sugar and eggs in medium bowl until blended. Beat in lemon juice, lemon peel, and baking powder, then remaining ¼ cup flour for filling.

Pour filling over hot crust. Bake until set in center and beginning to brown, about 20 minutes. Transfer pan to rack and cool. (*Can be made 1 day ahead. Cover; chill.*)

Cut pastry into 24 bars. Transfer to platter and dust with additional powdered sugar.

MAKES 24

Chocolate Macaroons

1⅓ cups mini semisweet chocolate chips (about 8 ounces), divided

2 large egg whites
¼ teaspoon salt
½ cup sugar
½ teaspoon vanilla extract
1½ cups sweetened flaked coconut

Preheat oven to 325°F. Line 2 large rimmed baking sheets with parchment paper. Place 1 cup chocolate chips in microwave-safe bowl; microwave on low setting at 10-second intervals until chocolate is melted, stirring occasionally. Cool just to room temperature.

Using electric mixer, beat egg whites and salt in medium bowl until soft peaks form.

Gradually add sugar, then vanilla, beating until whites are thick and glossy. Fold in melted chocolate and coconut, then remaining ⅓ cup chocolate chips.

Drop batter by heaping teaspoonfuls onto prepared sheets, spacing 1½ inches apart. Bake cookies 10 minutes. Reverse sheets. Bake until tops are dry and cracked and tester inserted into centers comes out with moist crumbs attached, about 10 minutes longer. Cool cookies on sheets on racks. Store airtight at room temperature up to 2 days.

MAKES ABOUT 30

Apricot-Orange Shortbread Bars

    1 cup apricot preserves
    3 tablespoons orange liqueur (such as Grand Marnier)

    1 cup (2 sticks) unsalted butter, room temperature
    ¾ cup sugar
    1 teaspoon almond extract
    2 cups all purpose flour
    ¼ teaspoon salt
    ¼ cup (packed) almond paste (from 7-ounce roll), crumbled
    ½ cup sliced almonds, divided

Preheat oven to 325°F. Butter 9x9x2-inch metal baking pan; line bottom and sides of pan with parchment paper, extending over sides. Butter parchment. Mix preserves and liqueur in small bowl; set aside.

Using electric mixer, beat butter and sugar in large bowl until well blended. Beat in extract. Add flour and salt; beat just until blended. Transfer 1 cup of dough to another small bowl; add crumbled almond paste and mix with fingertips until small clumps form. Mix in ¼ cup sliced almonds; set aside for topping.

Press remaining dough onto bottom of prepared pan. Spread preserves mixture over. Using fingertips, coarsely crumble topping over, then sprinkle with ¼ cup almonds. Press lightly into preserves.

Bake shortbread until top and crust edges are golden brown, about 1 hour. Cool in pan on rack. Using parchment paper as aid, lift shortbread from pan. Cut into 4 equal strips, then cut each strip crosswise into 8 small bar cookies. (*Can be prepared ahead. Store airtight in single layer at room temperature up to 4 days or freeze up to 2 weeks.*)

MAKES 32

Index

Page numbers in *italics* indicate color photographs.

Acknowledgments

RECIPES
Joy Ackerman
Bruce Aidells
Marielle Ainsworth
Baldpate Inn, Estes Park, Colorado
Sondra Bernstein
Lena Cederham Birnbaum
Boulettes Larder,
San Francisco, California
Kimberly Boyce
C & O, Charlottesville, Virginia
Carla Capalbo
Penelope Casas
Dalton Cole
Tom Colicchio
Cat Cora
Country Hermitage Bed &
Breakfast, Traverse City, Michigan
Lane Crowther
Lori De Mori
Joe Dion
Tom Douglas
Anitra Earle
Laura Evans
Elizabeth Falkner

Sara Foster
Francesca's North,
Northbrook, Illinois
Hugh Garvey
Daryl Getman
Maggie Glezer
Scott Goetz
Rozanne Gold
Eli Gorelick
Dorie Greenspan
Julie Hasson
Bev Heinecke
Evelyn Herring
Jill Silverman Hough
Doris Jacobson
Michele Anna Jordan
Jeanne Thiel Kelley
Judi Kerr
Kristine Kidd
Evan Kleiman
Annabel Langbein
Sue Lawrence
Lilette, New Orleans
Loaves & Fishes,
Sagaponack, New York

Susan Herrmann Loomis
Emily Luchetti
Janet Taylor McCracken
Molyvos, New York, NY
Luz Montez
Selma Brown Morrow
Musso & Frank,
Hollywood, California
Micol Negrin
Nancy Oakes
John Palacio
Kristi, Parnell
Sal Passalacqua
Paumanok Vineyards,
Aquebogue, New York
Mai Pham
Michael Presnal
Lisa and Stephen Price
Anna Pump
Jamie Purviance
Ted Reader
Victoria Abbott Riccardi
Judy Rodgers
Gemma Sanita Sciabica
Michele Scicolone

Marika and Gianluca Seguso
Shamiana, Kirkland, Washington
Marie Simmons
Maria Helm Sinskey
Deborah Snyder
Annette and Craig Wyrick-Solari
Sripraphai, New York, NY
Molly Stevens
Sarah Tenaglia
Alexis Watson
Dede Wilson
Yarrow Bay Beach Cafe,
Kirkland, Washington
Zoom, Park City, Utah

PHOTOGRAPHY
Sang An
Noel Barnhurst
Wyatt Counts
Fran Gealer
Leo Gong
Lisa Hubbard
Brian Leatart
Ellie Miller
Pornchai Mittongtare